# The ChatGpt Revolution - Unlock the Potential of AI

## Opportunities, Risks and Ways to Build an Automated Business in the Age of New Digital Media

BILL B. BROWN

# Contents

# EXCLUSIVE BONUS

Scan the QR code and
get 33 highly useful Chat GPT
prompts for free!

# Introduction

Many of us have encountered machines that think and behave like humans.

Artificial intelligence (AI) lies behind these technologies. Once a fringe concept in science fiction, AI has developed into one of the most transformative technologies of our modern era.

We now live in a world where smart devices like Amazon Alexa and Google Assistant can understand us and reply to our questions, where chatbots provide customer service without us having to speak to a human. And if we're honest, we've probably started taking it all for granted.

Let's set the scene for this book on ChatGPT by discussing AI and its intriguing path of evolution.

# What is Artificial Intelligence (AI)?

Artificial Intelligence (AI) is a broad field of computer science and engineering that focuses on creating intelligent machines that can perform tasks that typically require human-level intelligence.

These tasks include perception, reasoning, learning, decision-making, and natural language processing.

AI aims to create machines that can think, learn, and adapt like humans or even surpass human intelligence in some areas.

## Origins of AI

AI is not a new concept. The term "artificial intelligence" was first coined in the 1950s by computer scientist John McCarthy. However, it wasn't until the last few decades that AI made significant progress and became a buzzword in the technology industry.

Today, AI is used in a wide range of applications, from image and speech recognition to autonomous vehicles, virtual assistants, and medical diagnosis. As such, AI has the potential to revolutionize many industries and change the way we live and work – and this is already happening.

One of AI's most exciting applications is natural language processing (NLP) – and also the most relevant for exploring ChatGPT. NLP is a subfield of AI that focuses on the interaction between computers and humans through natural language. NLP is used in virtual assistants, chatbots, and language translation applications.

Chatbots are a great example of the power of NLP. Chatbots are computer programs that can simulate conversation with human users.

## Training

Machines are taught to understand language through a process called training. During training, machines are fed vast amounts of human language data, such as books, articles, and online content, allowing them to learn how language is used and how it can be interpreted.

Once a machine has been trained on language data, it can be used to perform a variety of language-related tasks. For example, a machine can be trained to recognize speech patterns and convert spoken language into text. It can also be trained to analyze text data, such as emails, social media posts, and news articles, to extract information and insights.

## Generating Language

Another essential aspect of natural language processing is language generation.

Machines can be trained to generate grammatically correct and semantically meaningful text. This allows machines to generate natural-sounding responses to queries and even create creative and original text, such as stories, jokes, and poetry.

You'll discover that ChatGPT is quite the comedian when asked!

# Introducing ChatGPT

ChatGPT is an AI language model developed by OpenAI that is trained on a massive dataset of human language, allowing it to understand and generate responses to a wide range of queries.

ChatGPT is designed to converse with humans, providing useful and informative responses to questions and queries. It can also generate creative and original text, such as stories, jokes, and poetry which don't appear anywhere else in the world.

One of the world's most famous examples of AI, ChatGPT is an example of the incredible potential of AI and natural language processing. It demonstrates how machines can be trained to understand and generate human language, opening up new possibilities for communication and interaction between humans and machines.

AI is a rapidly evolving field that has the potential to revolutionize many aspects of our lives – ChatGPT is one of many developments which will likely integrate themselves into our daily lives.

Let's take a brief look at how we got to where we are today.

## Early 2000s: The Start of Machine Learning and Language Processing

In the early 2000s, researchers began using machine learning techniques for natural language processing (NLP) tasks.

NLP is one of AI's main disciplines, or umbrellas, and is concerned with teaching AIs how to understand human language.

After all, language is one of the many facets of our existence that defines us. It enables us to communicate and share everything from knowledge to emotions and feelings.

Early AI researchers applied different methods to tasks like text classification and understanding the feelings behind texts (sentiment analysis).

Early NLP applications included spam filters and search engines based on keywords.

## Late 2000s: The Arrival of Deep Learning

The late 2000s witnessed the arrival of deep learning, which uses artificial neural networks with many layers to process and learn from data. Neural networks are modeled on the human brain.

Researchers started using deep learning techniques for NLP tasks, leading to the development of Word2Vec in 2013.

Word2Vec was a game-changer because it allowed computers to understand the relationships between words, paving the way for more advanced NLP models.

## Mid-2010s: The Development of Sequence-to-Sequence Models

In the mid-2010s, sequence-to-sequence (seq2seq) models were developed, allowing for more complex NLP tasks like translating languages and summarizing texts.

This led to a rapid increase in the effectiveness and accuracy of tools like Google Translate.

## Late 2010s: The Introduction of Transformers and Transfer Learning

The late 2010s marked a significant change in NLP with the introduction of the Transformer architecture in 2017.

Transformers are a new generation of technologies designed to support high-tech AIs, like ChatGPT.

## Early 2020s: The Rise of Large Language Models

The early 2020s saw the rise of LLMs like GPT-3, which pushed the limits of NLP by training on massive amounts of data and using billions of parameters.

These models demonstrated incredible capabilities, including learning from just a few examples and generating human-like text.

LLMs mark a new era in NLP – as we can see from the rise of ChatGPT – the most famous LLM right now.

AI systems can now engage in contextually relevant conversations and perform a wide range of tasks.

# Enter: ChatGPT

The GPT series started with the first version, simply named GPT-1. Created by tech company OpenAI, this language model used the Transformer architecture as its foundation.

Think of it like a complex structure made of smaller, connecting pieces – the Transformer is the blueprint that guides how those pieces fit together. This architecture enabled GPT-1 to process text more effectively than older, less efficient methods.

GPT-1 showed solid language abilities but was limited in understanding and creativity.

OpenAI knew it could improve, so they developed the next version: GPT-2.

This model was stronger, with more parameters that allowed it to learn and process complex language patterns. GPT-2 generated more coherent and relevant text than before.

However, with this power came concerns about potential misuse, such as creating disinformation or spam. As a result, OpenAI decided to withhold the full release of GPT-2, focusing on developing a safer, more advanced language model.

GPT-3 was a significant advancement in the GPT series. Its parameters increased to a massive 175 billion, greatly improving its contextual understanding. This allowed GPT-3 to perform tasks with little prompting, known as "few-shot learning."

OpenAI aimed to push the boundaries even further, leading to the development of GPT-4.

# How Does ChatGPT Work?

To make ChatGPT a versatile and knowledgeable AI, it needs to be fed with an incredible amount of text data.

**Understanding how ChatGPT knows what it knows is absolutely vital to using the tool.**

## Training Data

The training data comes from a wide array of sources, including books, articles, and websites, covering a multitude of topics.

This rich data set allows ChatGPT to learn the intricacies of human language, common phrases, and even cultural references.

Think of it as a librarian of the most extensive library in the world, which has read and remembered every single book.

While this might seem like an exaggeration, there are billions or even trillions of words in ChatGPT's training data. OpenAI hasn't disclosed exactly how much data is used.

It's important to remember that ChatGPT is limited by its training data. It also lacks knowledge past September 2021, so it's inherently outdated. Information past this point does not appear in its training data.

Bizarrely, ChatGPT doesn't even know about GPT-4, even though it can use it today.

As an AI language model with a knowledge cutoff in September 2021, I don't have the ability
to verify real-time information or events. If GPT-4 has been released since my last update, I
wouldn't be aware of it. I encourage you to check official sources or news from OpenAI to
verify the current status of GPT-4 or any other subsequent models.

## Preparing for the Real World: Pre-training and Fine-tuning

The training process for ChatGPT consists of two main stages: pre-training and fine-tuning.

During pre-training, the model is exposed to vast text data and learns to predict what comes next in a sentence. This helps ChatGPT grasp the structure of language and build a strong foundation.

Once the foundation is laid, it's time for fine-tuning. In this stage, ChatGPT is refined using a more specific dataset containing examples of human-generated text and responses.

This dataset may include conversations or prompts that people have shared, ensuring the AI can engage in meaningful and relevant conversations with users like you.

## The Result: A Conversational AI That Understands You

The combination of diverse training data and a meticulous two-step training process enables ChatGPT to understand and generate human-like responses.

As a result, it can answer your questions, engage in meaningful conversations, and even provide creative input when needed.

So, the next time you interact with ChatGPT, remember that it has been carefully crafted through an extensive training process.

# Understand the OpenAI Business Model

**It's crucial to understand how OpenAI has built such a powerful tool.**

While most people are familiar with ChatGPT as a tool accessible through the web, OpenAI generates revenue primarily through its Application Programming Interface (API), which allows businesses and developers to access and integrate its AI models, such as ChatGPT, into their own applications, products, or services.

OpenAI essentially sells the model to other businesses. So, OpenAI monetizes its cutting-edge AI research and development by providing the API as a paid service.

Here's how businesses can use OpenAI's technology through the API:

1. **Integration**: OpenAI's API enables businesses to incorporate the AI model into their existing systems or applications. This can be achieved by making API calls from the business's platform, which allows them to utilize the AI's capabilities directly within their products or services.

2. **Customization**: The API allows businesses to tailor the AI model to their specific needs by providing custom prompts, adjusting parameters, or even fine-tuning the model on their own datasets (subject to OpenAI's guidelines and support).

3. **Scalability**: By using OpenAI's API, businesses can access powerful AI models without investing in expensive hardware or infrastructure. OpenAI manages the underlying infrastructure and ensures that the API is highly available, enabling businesses to scale their usage as needed.

4.  **Rapid development**: With access to pre-trained models through the API, businesses can accelerate their AI development process, as they don't need to build and train models from scratch. This allows for quicker deployment of AI-powered features and services.

Some common use cases of OpenAI in business or commercial contexts include:

- AI chatbots for customer support, sales, or onboarding
- Content generation and editing for digital marketing or publishing
- Personalized recommendations in e-commerce or content platforms
- Data analysis, visualization, and report generation
- Automating repetitive tasks, such as data entry, filtering, or sorting
- AI-based assistants for professionals, such as programmers, writers, or designers

By offering an API, OpenAI enables businesses across various industries to leverage its advanced AI models, driving innovation and creating new possibilities for AI-powered applications and solutions.

**This is what supports the free version of ChatGPT.**

# Basic Use Cases of GPT

Let's take a look at some fundamental examples of how ChatGPT is used before delving into more specific use cases:

1. **Social media management**: ChatGPT can help businesses manage their social media presence by crafting tailored, engaging posts for various platforms. It can create promotional content, draft responses to customer inquiries, and generate relevant content to keep followers informed and entertained.

2. **Personalized virtual assistants**: ChatGPT can act as a personalized virtual assistant, understanding user preferences and needs to provide customized support. It can engage in context-aware conversations to help users with various tasks, such as managing their schedules, setting reminders, booking appointments, and even suggesting personalized entertainment options based on their interests.

3. **Writing assistance**: ChatGPT excels in writing. Aspiring writers can use ChatGPT to overcome writer's block or generate new ideas for stories. ChatGPT can create character backstories, plot outlines, or even draft entire scenes by providing a brief description or a set of keywords. It can also help with editing and refining content by suggesting improvements in grammar, style, and tone. This extends to academic and technical writing.

4. **Educational support**: ChatGPT is a valuable learning tool, offering on-demand assistance to students in various subjects. It can answer questions, provide explanations, and even generate quizzes or practice problems based on

the student's needs. This personalized learning experience can help students overcome challenges and gain a deeper understanding of the subject matter.

5. **Math and programming:** ChatGPT, especially the GPT4 model, is exceptionally efficient at math and programming tasks, including building algorithms, writing code, and solving complex equations.

6. **Summarization**: ChatGPT can help users stay informed by summarizing articles from multiple sources. It can generate concise summaries that retain essential information, allowing users to quickly grasp the main points of an article without needing to read the entire piece.

7. **Resume and cover letter writing**: Job seekers can use ChatGPT to create well-written, targeted resumes and cover letters. By providing relevant information about their work experience, skills, and the desired position, ChatGPT can generate documents that highlight the job seeker's qualifications and make them stand out to potential employers.

8. **Travel planning**: ChatGPT can serve as a virtual travel assistant, suggesting destinations, attractions, and activities based on user preferences. It can also provide information on local customs, transportation options, and even recommend restaurants or accommodations. ChatGPT can help users plan memorable and enjoyable trips by offering personalized recommendations and insights.

# What Are The Advantages of Using ChatGPT?

ChatGPT is a powerful informational tool.

Here are some of its fundamental advantages which have made it so popular:

1. **Natural language understanding**: ChatGPT has a deep understanding of human language, which allows it to comprehend context, nuances, and complex phrasings. This makes it suitable for a wide range of tasks that require human-like language comprehension and generation.

2. **Versatility**: ChatGPT can be applied to various use cases across multiple industries, including customer support, content creation, software development, e-commerce, and more. Its adaptability allows businesses to address different challenges using a single AI model.

3. **High-quality content generation**: ChatGPT can generate coherent, contextually relevant, and grammatically accurate content. This makes it valuable for tasks that require content creation, such as drafting articles, writing social media posts, or generating product descriptions.

4. **Time and cost savings:** ChatGPT can help businesses save time and reduce labor costs by automating tasks that traditionally require human intervention. This enables organizations to allocate resources more effectively and focus on higher-priority tasks.

5. **Enhanced user experience**: Integrating ChatGPT into user-facing applications, such as chatbots or virtual assistants, can lead to more engaging and personalized user experiences, ultimately increasing customer satisfaction and loyalty.

6. **Scalability**: ChatGPT can handle many requests simultaneously, allowing businesses to scale their AI-powered solutions as needed without significant investments in infrastructure or resources.

7. **Continuous improvement**: As an AI model developed by OpenAI, ChatGPT benefits from ongoing research and development efforts. This ensures that the model keeps improving, incorporating new knowledge and capabilities.

**Let's move onto accessing and using ChatGPT.**

# How to Access ChatGPT

### Step 1: Visit the OpenAI website

To begin sign-up, navigate to the OpenAI website (https://www.openai.com/) using your preferred web browser.

On the main page, you'll find information about ChatGPT, as well as other AI products and services offered by OpenAI.

### Step 2: Locate the ChatGPT section

Scroll through the homepage until you find the section dedicated to ChatGPT. You may also use the site's search function or navigate directly to the ChatGPT page (https://www.openai.com/chatgpt) if available.

### Step 3: Click on "Sign Up" or "Get Started"

Once you've reached the ChatGPT section or page, look for a "Sign Up" or "Get Started" button. Clicking on this button will take you to the registration page.

### Step 4: Complete the registration form

On the registration page, you'll be asked to provide personal information such as your name, email address, and desired password. You can sign-up with Google or other accounts.

Make sure to use a valid email address, as you'll need to confirm it later. You may also be asked to agree to the terms of service and privacy policy. After completing the form, click the "Submit" or "Register" button.

## Step 5: Confirm your email address

Shortly after submitting your registration, you should receive a confirmation email. Open the email and click on the verification link provided. This step is crucial to activating your ChatGPT account.

## Step 6: Choose a subscription plan

After confirming your email address, you may be prompted to select a subscription plan for ChatGPT. You can sign-up to the premium plan for $20/mo as of mid-2023.

## Step 7: Access ChatGPT

Once your payment is processed (if applicable), you'll be granted access to ChatGPT.

You can now start exploring its features and leveraging its AI capabilities in your projects or daily tasks.

# Using ChatGPT

**To use ChatGPT effectively, it's essential to understand the role of prompts and how to engineer them to get the desired results.**

Prompts are the inputs you feed into ChatGPT, much like the inputs you feed into a search engine. However, they can be significantly longer and more complex.

You write these into the tool.

The process of designing props is called prompt engineering.

Here's a guide to help you make the most of ChatGPT and master the art of prompt engineering:

**Be clear and concise**: When creating a prompt for ChatGPT, make sure your instructions are clear and concise. Clearly state the task you want the model to perform or the information you're looking for. This helps the model understand your requirements and generate an accurate response.

**Use examples**: When possible, provide examples to guide ChatGPT's response. This technique, known as few-shot learning, helps the model understand the format or style you're looking for. For instance, if you want ChatGPT to generate a list of movie recommendations in a specific genre, provide some examples to set the context.

**Specify the desired format**: If you have a specific format in mind for ChatGPT's response, make sure to mention it in your prompt. For example, if you want a summary of an article, you could ask, "Please provide a concise summary of the following article in 3-4 sentences."

**Use step-by-step instructions**: For complex tasks, break down your prompt into step-by-step instructions. This helps ChatGPT process the information more effectively and ensures that it addresses each aspect of the task.

**Experiment with different prompts**: ChatGPT's performance can vary depending on the prompt. If you don't get the desired output on the first attempt, rephrase your prompt or provide additional context. Experimenting with different prompts can help you discover the best approach to elicit the most accurate and relevant response.

**Limit the response length**: If you want a shorter response, specify the desired length in your prompt. For example, you could ask for a "one-sentence summary" or a "50-word explanation" to ensure the output is concise and focused.

**Set the appropriate tone**: If you want ChatGPT to generate content with a specific tone, such as formal, casual, or humorous, mention it explicitly in your prompt. This helps the model adjust its writing style to match your requirements.

**Iterate and refine**: Prompt engineering is an iterative process. As you work with ChatGPT, you'll gain a better understanding of the model's strengths and limitations. Use this knowledge to refine your prompts, adjusting your approach to get the best results.

**Now, it's important to understand the difference between GPT3 and GPT4.**

# EXCLUSIVE BONUS

## Scan the QR code and get 33 highly useful Chat GPT prompts for free!

# GPT3 vs GPT4

On April 14, 2023, OpenAI unveiled GPT-4, the next-generation successor to GPT-3. These are the AI models behind ChatGPT.

## Feature comparison

**Parameters:** In language model terminology, "parameters" denote adjustable internal settings or variables that facilitate learning and text generation. Generally, more parameters signify a more robust and capable model.

When comparing GPT-3 and GPT-4, it's essential to consider the parameters on which these language models are built. GPT-3 was launched with 175 billion parameters, making it one of the largest Large Language Models (LLMs). GPT-4 is rumored to offer 10x that amount.

**Implications:** A higher parameter count implies the model can better learn and generalize patterns from the data it processes, resulting in more coherent, contextually relevant, and fitting text generation. GPT-4 is essentially better at everything, but slower as a result.

While ChatGPT powered by GPT-3 is currently free, OpenAI has introduced its latest and most advanced GPT-4 model as part of its $20 monthly subscription package.

For existing subscribers to ChatGPT Plus, upgrading from the GPT-3.5 default and legacy model to GPT-4 is available, enabling users to toggle between both versions.

See below.

| Model<br>Default (GPT-3.5) | ⌄ |
| --- | --- |
| Default (GPT-3.5) | ✓ |
| GPT-4 | |
| Legacy (GPT-3.5) | |

ChatGPT PLUS

This feature allows you to fully experience and appreciate the enhanced capabilities of the GPT-4 iteration.

If you've been experimenting with GPT-3.5 and wish to unleash the full force of what ChatGPT has to offer, consider subscribing to Plus. Subscribing also reduces the likelihood of being disconnected from the session, and is generally more reliable.

**So, is ChatGPT free? Yes, but you could call OpenAI's model "freemium" now they've released GPT-4 for paid subscribers only!**

# Before You Start: Top 10 Tips for Using ChatGPT

Before we move on with worked examples of ChatGPT in action, let's run over 10 tips to bear in mind when using the tool:

1. **Be specific**: Provide clear and detailed information when asking questions or making requests to help ChatGPT understand your needs and provide accurate responses.

2. **Experiment with phrasing**: If you're unsatisfied with the response, try rephrasing your query or providing more context to get the desired answer.

3. **Use step-by-step instructions**: When asking for explanations or guidance, request step-by-step instructions to get a more structured and organized response.

4. **Set limitations**: If you want a brief or concise response, specify a word or sentence limit to guide the AI in delivering a more focused answer.

5. **Verify information**: As ChatGPT's knowledge is updated until September 2021, always double-check the information provided, especially for recent events or advancements. It's not always right. This is very important when dealing with factual or sensitive information.

6. **Ask follow-up questions**: If you're not satisfied with the initial response or need more information, don't hesitate to ask follow-up questions to get the desired answer.

7. **Be patient**: ChatGPT may sometimes require a few attempts to understand complex or unusual queries. If you encounter such issues, try breaking down the question or providing more context.

8. **Utilize multi-part questions**: When you need information on multiple aspects of a topic, ask multi-part questions to get more comprehensive answers.

9. **Leverage creativity:** ChatGPT can generate creative content such as stories, poems, or marketing ideas. Feel free to explore these capabilities for your creative needs.

10. **Provide feedback**: Providing feedback on the AI's responses helps improve its performance over time. Don't hesitate to share your thoughts if you encounter an issue or have suggestions.

# Let's Go! ChatGPT in Action

**Here, we'll investigate some of the many uses of ChatGPT to get your inspiration flowing.**

Once you're familiar with the tool, developing your own ideas and workflows will become easy.

## Use Case 1: Education and Learning

**ChatGPT is essentially a 24/7 tutor tailored to your exact requirements.**

Since it's learned from billions of pieces of text, it acts as an AI librarian and tutor that can look virtually anything up.

Get the Support You Need, When You Need It

Struggling with a difficult topic and need help?

ChatGPT offers instant feedback and guidance. It can answer questions and engage in meaningful conversations, making learning enjoyable and interactive.

Stay Motivated with Your Very Own Study Buddy

ChatGPT acts as a buddy or companion for thousands of students worldwide, providing companionship and helping them stay focused.

Test your understanding of concepts, practice problem-solving, or even prepare for exams with quizzes and flashcards,

### Master New Languages with Confidence

If you're looking to learn a new language, ChatGPT can be your ultimate language-learning assistant.

Practice conversational skills, receive feedback on grammar and pronunciation, and expand your vocabulary through real-time conversations.

### Unleash Your Creativity and Critical Thinking

Ready to think outside the box? ChatGPT can help you develop essential problem-solving and creative thinking skills.

Brainstorm ideas, explore different perspectives, and even create stories or poems together. By engaging with ChatGPT, you'll be challenged to think critically and creatively.

## Example 1: Topic Summarization

ChatGPT is extremely effective at summarizing topics. It can do this for practically anything, and at any level.

Here is ChatGPT's response to the prompt: *explain quantum theory to a 12-year-old:*

 Quantum theory is a set of ideas in science that explains how the smallest particles in the universe, like atoms and electrons, behave. These tiny particles act differently than larger things we see and touch every day. In the quantum world, particles can be in more than one place at the same time, and they can also act like both particles and waves. Scientists use quantum theory to understand and predict how these tiny particles interact with each other, which helps us make new technology like computers and lasers. It's a fascinating and strange part of science that challenges our everyday understanding of how things work.

Now, here is the response to *explain quantum theory to a physics graduate:*

Quantum theory, or quantum mechanics, is a fundamental framework in physics that describes the behavior of matter and energy at the atomic and subatomic scale. It deviates from classical mechanics, as it introduces the principles of quantization, wave-particle duality, superposition, and entanglement.

At the heart of quantum theory is the concept of quantization, which asserts that certain physical quantities, such as energy levels of electrons in atoms, are discrete rather than continuous. This led to the development of the Schrödinger equation, a partial differential equation that governs the wave function of a quantum system, and the Heisenberg uncertainty principle, which states that there is a fundamental limit to the precision with which certain pairs of physical properties can be known simultaneously.

Wave-particle duality is another key aspect of quantum mechanics, as it proposes that particles, like electrons and photons, exhibit both wave-like and particle-like behavior. This is exemplified by the famous double-slit experiment, where particles can create an interference pattern when passing through two slits, just as waves would.

Superposition is a principle that allows particles to exist in multiple states simultaneously until a measurement is made, at which point the particle's state collapses to a single outcome. This is the basis for the famous thought experiment of Schrödinger's cat, illustrating the seemingly paradoxical nature of quantum mechanics.

Lastly, quantum entanglement is a phenomenon where particles become correlated in such a way that the state of one particle instantly affects the state of another, regardless of the distance between them. This phenomenon has been experimentally demonstrated and is central to the development of quantum technologies such as quantum computing and quantum communication.

As we can see, ChatGPT does an excellent job of explaining this highly complex topic and tailors the response precisely to your knowledge level and requirements.

We can also demonstrate this with history. Here is the response to *describe the battle of Thermopylae*

The Battle of Thermopylae took place in 480 BCE during the Greco-Persian Wars. It was fought between an alliance of Greek city-states, led by King Leonidas I of Sparta, and the Persian Empire, led by King Xerxes I. The battle occurred at the narrow coastal passage of Thermopylae in central Greece.

The Persian army, which greatly outnumbered the Greek forces, sought to invade and conquer Greece. King Leonidas led a small force of around 7,000 Greek soldiers, including 300 Spartans, to defend the pass of Thermopylae, which served as a strategic bottleneck.

The Greek forces used the narrow terrain to their advantage, holding off the vastly larger Persian army for three days. However, a local resident named Ephialtes betrayed the Greeks by revealing a mountain path that allowed the Persians to outflank and surround the defenders.

Realizing their position had been compromised, Leonidas dismissed most of his troops to save their lives, while he and his 300 Spartans, along with a few hundred other Greeks, remained to fight to the death. The Greeks were ultimately defeated, but their valiant stand at Thermopylae allowed the other Greek city-states time to prepare for the Persian invasion, which later led to key Greek victories and the eventual withdrawal of Persian forces. The Battle of Thermopylae has since become a symbol of courage and sacrifice against overwhelming odds.

From here, you can quiz ChatGPT on certain aspects of the text, such as asking who King Leonidas was or even asking how accurate the popular account of the battle is.

You can use ChatGPT as a skeptic, asking it to delve into facts and try to question their legitimacy. However, it's also sensible to be skeptical of ChatGPT, as it's prone to misappropriating information.

Here's another example. If you're taking your car in for repair, you could ask ChatGPT, *list the main costs of car servicing and repair*

Here's a table of estimated car repair costs for various common issues. Please note that  these are approximate values and can vary depending on the make, model, and location.

| Repair / Service | Estimated Cost ($) |
| --- | --- |
| Oil Change | 30 - 70 |
| Brake Pad Replacement | 100 - 300 |
| Brake Rotor Replacement | 200 - 600 |
| Battery Replacement | 100 - 200 |
| Alternator Replacement | 300 - 600 |
| Starter Replacement | 200 - 500 |
| Spark Plug Replacement | 100 - 200 |
| Timing Belt Replacement | 400 - 900 |

As we can see, ChatGPT returns a table of costs. This draws attention to ChatGPT's abilities to create tables from scratch.

## Example 2: Language Learning

While most of ChatGPT's training data is written in English, it speaks over 27 languages, including English, Spanish, French, German, Italian, Dutch, Portuguese, Chinese (Mandarin), Japanese, Korean, Russian, Arabic, Hebrew, Swedish, Danish, Norwegian, Finnish, Turkish, Polish, Hungarian, Czech, Greek, Hindi, Bengali, Indonesian, Thai, and Vietnamese.

It's important to note that performance varies between languages.

For language learning, it's an immensely powerful tool, enabling you to translate information between languages and interact with it in your native language.

Here are some ideas:

1. **Conversation practice:** You can engage with ChatGPT in real-time conversations in your target language, helping you improve your speaking and comprehension skills by simulating interactions with native speakers.

2. **Grammar and vocabulary**: ChatGPT can provide explanations and examples of grammar rules and help you expand your vocabulary with new words and phrases, making it easier for you to grasp the language structure and express yourself more fluently.

3. **Pronunciation feedback**: Although ChatGPT cannot hear you, you can type out words or phrases phonetically, and the AI can correct any errors, guiding you toward proper pronunciation and helping you sound more natural when speaking your target language.

4. **Cultural insights**: ChatGPT can share information about the culture, customs, and history of the countries where your target language is spoken, giving you a deeper understanding and appreciation of the language and enriching your learning experience.

5. **Reading comprehension**: You can practice reading skills by sharing a passage or article in your target language with ChatGPT. The AI can help you understand its meaning, explain unfamiliar vocabulary, and discuss the main ideas, enhancing your ability to interpret written content.

6. **Writing assistance**: ChatGPT can help you improve your writing skills in your target language by providing feedback on your written work, suggesting better phrasing or vocabulary, and offering guidance on proper sentence structure and punctuation.

7. **Language exercises and quizzes**: ChatGPT can generate language exercises, such as fill-in-the-blank, multiple-choice questions, or translation tasks, to help you reinforce your understanding of grammar, vocabulary, etc.

8. **Idiomatic expressions**: ChatGPT can introduce you to common idiomatic expressions and slang used by native speakers, enabling you to communicate more naturally and understand the nuances of everyday speech in your target language.

Here's ChatGPT's response to: *tell me how traditional Japanese noodles are made*

 Of course! Here's a brief description of how traditional Japanese noodles are made:

日本の伝統的な麺の作り方について説明します。主な日本の麺料理には、うどん、そば、ラーメンがあります。これらの麺は、異なる製法と原料を使用しています。

1. うどん: うどんは、小麦粉、水、塩を混ぜて作られます。まず、小麦粉に塩水を加えて生地を練ります。次に、生地を薄く伸ばし、包丁で細長く切って形を整えます。最後に、切った麺を湯で茹で、冷水で冷やした後、つゆや具材と一緒に食べます。

2. そば: そばは、そば粉（そばの実を挽いたもの）と水を混ぜて作られます。生地を練り、薄く伸ばし、うどんと同様に細長く切ります。茹でたそばは、ざるそばとして冷水で冷やして食べたり、かけそばとして熱いつゆに浸けて食べます。

3. ラーメン: ラーメンの麺は、小麦粉、水、塩、かんすい（アルカリ性の水）を混ぜて作られます。生地を練り、伸ばし、細長く切ります。茹でた麺は、豚骨、醤油、味噌などのスープと具材と共に提供されます。

日本の伝統的な麺は、素朴な味わいと独特の食感が特徴で、日本料理の要素の一つとして世界中で愛されています。

You might be wondering how you can get ChatGPT to provide you with language-learning quizzes. Simply ask it.

# Here's the response to *Language exercises and quizzes: show me an example for learning English*

 Certainly! Here's an example of a fill-in-the-blank exercise for learning English:

Complete the following sentences with the appropriate form of the verb in parentheses:

1. She _____ (be) at the library yesterday.
2. If I _____ (have) more time, I would travel more often.
3. I _____ (cook) dinner when the phone rang.
4. By the time we arrived, the movie _____ (start).
5. They _____ (live) in Paris for five years before moving to London.

Once you've filled in the blanks, I can provide the correct answers and explanations if needed. This is just one example of how ChatGPT can create interactive language exercises to help improve your English skills.

## Want to make it harder? Simply ask.

 Sure, here's a more challenging exercise involving English idioms and advanced vocabulary.
Fill in the blanks with the appropriate words or phrases:

1. She's trying to _____ the issue, but we need to address it head-on.
2. Despite his best efforts, John couldn't _____ the criticism he received.
3. The meeting was _____, as no one came prepared with the necessary information.
4. After her promotion, she felt like she was _____, finally getting the recognition she deserved.
5. The author's use of _____ language made the text difficult to understand for some readers.

This exercise requires a deeper understanding of English idioms and advanced vocabulary, making it more challenging. Once you've filled in the blanks, I can provide the correct answers and explanations if needed.

# Example 3: Essay writing and Academia

Academic writing can be challenging, but with ChatGPT, you can elevate essays and research projects to new heights.

ChatGPT is a powerful AI language model that offers valuable assistance throughout the entire writing process.

**Beware** – AI-written essays have come under fire from schools and universities worldwide. There are ways to determine if an essay has been generated. Plus, teachers will likely learn the signs of how to spot an AI-generated essay. Lastly, ChatGPT does have a habit of "hallucinating" information that isn't 100% correct, which can give students away.

Brainstorming Ideas and Formulating Thesis Statements

Starting with a blank page can be daunting, but ChatGPT can help you brainstorm ideas and develop compelling thesis statements. Simply provide a general topic or question, and the AI can generate a list of potential angles or arguments to explore in your essay.

This creative input can help you refine your focus and construct a strong foundation for your writing.

Here's the response for *come up with some ideas for studies surrounding social media usage at Master's level*

1. The impact of social media on mental health and well-being: A longitudinal study examining the relationship between social media usage patterns and psychological well-being among young adults.
2. The role of social media in political discourse and polarization: Investigating the effects of social media algorithms on the formation and reinforcement of political beliefs and the potential for echo chambers.
3. The influence of social media influencers on consumer behavior: Analyzing the effectiveness of influencer marketing campaigns and the factors that contribute to their success in driving consumer decision-making.
4. Social media and crisis communication: A comparative study of how organizations use social media platforms during crises to disseminate information, manage public relations, and maintain stakeholder trust.
5. The ethics of data privacy in social media platforms: Examining the implications of data collection practices and targeted advertising on user privacy, and exploring potential regulatory frameworks for protecting user information.
6. Social media and its impact on interpersonal communication: Investigating how social media usage affects face-to-face communication, relationship building, and social skills among different age groups.

## Structuring and Organizing Your Essay

A well-organized essay is essential for effective communication.

ChatGPT can offer suggestions on structuring your essay, including organizing your arguments, determining the flow of information, and creating coherent paragraphs.

By helping you outline your ideas, ChatGPT ensures that your essay is logically organized and easy to follow.

### Research Assistance and Fact-Checking

Navigating the vast world of academic resources can be overwhelming.

ChatGPT can assist you in finding reputable sources, summarizing key findings, and identifying relevant data to support your arguments.

Additionally, the AI can help you fact-check information to ensure your essay is accurate and well-informed.

## Improving Writing Style and Tone

Effective academic writing requires clarity, precision, and a formal tone.

ChatGPT can guide writing style, helping you choose appropriate vocabulary and sentence structures.

The AI can also review your work for consistency in tone and suggest improvements to make your writing more engaging and persuasive.

## Editing and Proofreading

Grammar, punctuation, and spelling errors can detract from your essay's credibility.

ChatGPT can help you identify and correct these mistakes, ensuring your writing is polished and professional.

Additionally, the AI can offer suggestions for rephrasing sentences to improve clarity and conciseness.

## Citation and Formatting Assistance

Proper citation and formatting are crucial in academic writing.

ChatGPT can help you adhere to specific citation styles, such as APA, MLA, or Chicago, and offer guidance on formatting your essay according to academic standards.

In-Depth Example: Diabetes Essay

Here is ChatGPT's output to *write an essay on diabetes with references*

Note the references used in the essay.

**Title: Understanding Diabetes: Types, Risk Factors, and Management Strategies**

**Introduction**

*Diabetes is a chronic health condition characterized by elevated blood sugar levels due to the body's inability to produce or effectively use insulin, a hormone responsible for regulating glucose levels (American Diabetes Association, 2021).*

*This essay will discuss the different types of diabetes, the risk factors associated with the condition, and the management strategies for maintaining optimal health in individuals with diabetes.*

**Types of Diabetes**

*There are three main types of diabetes: type 1, type 2, and gestational diabetes.*

*Type 1 diabetes, also known as insulin-dependent diabetes, is an autoimmune condition where the body's immune system attacks and destroys insulin-producing cells in the pancreas, leading to little or no insulin production (Mayo Clinic, 2021). This form of diabetes typically develops in childhood or adolescence but can also occur in adulthood.*

Type 2 diabetes, the most common form of diabetes, is characterized by the body's resistance to insulin or inadequate insulin production (CDC, 2021). This type of diabetes is often associated with lifestyle factors such as poor diet, lack of exercise, and obesity.

Gestational diabetes develops during pregnancy and typically resolves after the baby is born (National Institute of Diabetes and Digestive and Kidney Diseases, 2017). However, women who experience gestational diabetes are at an increased risk of developing type 2 diabetes later in life.

## Risk Factors

Several risk factors are associated with the development of diabetes, including genetic predisposition, obesity, sedentary lifestyle, and dietary habits (CDC, 2021). Family history plays a significant role in the likelihood of developing diabetes, with individuals having a higher risk if they have a parent or sibling with the condition (American Diabetes Association, 2021). Moreover, environmental factors such as exposure to certain viruses, like enteroviruses, may contribute to the development of type 1 diabetes (Laitinen et al., 2014).

## Management Strategies

Diabetes management involves a combination of lifestyle modifications, medication, and regular monitoring of blood sugar levels to prevent complications and maintain overall health. The following strategies are crucial for managing diabetes:

**Diet**: A balanced diet that is rich in fruits, vegetables, whole grains, lean proteins, and healthy fats can help regulate blood sugar levels and manage weight (American Diabetes Association, 2021).

**Physical Activity**: *Regular exercise, such as walking, swimming, or cycling, can help lower blood sugar levels and improve insulin sensitivity (Colberg et al., 2016).*

**Medication**: *Depending on the type and severity of diabetes, individuals may require insulin injections, oral medications, or other injectable medications to manage blood sugar levels (Mayo Clinic, 2021).*

**Blood Sugar Monitoring**: *Regularly monitoring blood sugar levels is essential for adjusting treatment plans and preventing complications (American Diabetes Association, 2021).*

**Education and Support**: *Ongoing education and support from healthcare professionals, family, and peers can help individuals with diabetes better understand their condition and manage their health effectively (Powers et al., 2017).*

## Conclusion

*Diabetes is a complex health condition with various types, risk factors, and management strategies. Understanding these aspects is crucial for preventing and managing the disease, improving the quality of life for individuals with diabetes, and reducing the risk of complications. By adopting healthy lifestyle habits, staying informed, and working closely with healthcare professionals, people with diabetes can effectively manage their condition and maintain overall health.*

## References

American Diabetes Association. (2021). Introduction: Standards of Medical Care in Diabetes—2021. Diabetes Care, 44(Supplement 1), S1-S2. https://doi.org/10.2337/dc21-S

CDC. (2021). Types of Diabetes. Centers for Disease Control and Prevention. Retrieved from https://www.cdc.gov/diabetes/basics/diabetes.html

Colberg, S. R., Sigal, R. J., Yardley, J. E., Riddell, M. C., Dunstan, D. W., Dempsey, P. C., ... & Tate, D. F. (2016). Physical Activity/Exercise and Diabetes: A Position Statement of the American Diabetes Association. Diabetes Care, 39(11), 2065-2079. https://doi.org/10.2337/dc16-1728

Laitinen, O. H., Honkanen, H., Pakkanen, O., Oikarinen, S., Hankaniemi, M. M., Huhtala, H., ... & Hyöty, H. (2014). Coxsackievirus B1 is associated with induction of β-cell autoimmunity that portends type 1 diabetes. Diabetes, 63(2), 446-455. https://doi.org/10.2337/db13-0619

Mayo Clinic. (2021). Diabetes. Retrieved from https://www.mayoclinic.org/diseases-conditions/diabetes/symptoms-causes/syc-20371444

National Institute of Diabetes and Digestive and Kidney Diseases. (2017). Gestational Diabetes. Retrieved from https://www.niddk.nih.gov/health-information/diabetes/overview/what-is-diabetes/gestational

Powers, M. A., Bardsley, J., Cypress, M., Duker, P., Funnell, M. M., Fischl, A. H., ... & Vivian, E. (2017). Diabetes self-management education and support in type 2 diabetes: a joint position statement of the American Diabetes Association, the American Association of Diabetes Educators, and the Academy of Nutrition and Dietetics. Diabetes Care, 40(7), 706-710. https://doi.org/10.2337/dci17-0025

## Example 5: Brainstorming

One of the ways that ChatGPT can be used is to help people brainstorm. Brainstorming is a process of generating creative ideas through a group discussion or individual reflection.

It's a valuable tool for problem-solving, innovation, and creativity. ChatGPT can provide a unique perspective on brainstorming by offering creative prompts, new ideas, and different approaches to problems.

To illustrate how ChatGPT can help with brainstorming, let's take the example of a writer struggling to develop ideas for a new story. The writer has hit a creative block and is feeling frustrated and stuck. So they decide to use ChatGPT to help them brainstorm.

The writer begins by typing a message to ChatGPT, asking for help developing ideas for a new story. ChatGPT responds with a prompt:

*"Imagine a world where humans have evolved to communicate telepathically. How would this affect the way they interact with each other and with the world around them?"*

The writer is intrigued by this idea and begins to explore it further.

They ask ChatGPT for more information about the world and its characters. ChatGPT responds with additional prompts and ideas:
- "What if the telepathic ability only worked between certain groups of people, creating a division between those who have the ability and those who don't?"
- "What if the telepathic ability had unintended consequences, such as the loss of privacy and the ability to keep secrets?"

- "What if there was a conflict between those who had the telepathic ability and those who didn't, leading to a struggle for power and control?"

The writer begins to build a story around these ideas, exploring the themes of power, control, and communication in a telepathic world. They ask ChatGPT for feedback on their ideas, and ChatGPT responds with constructive criticism and additional suggestions.

Through the conversation with ChatGPT, the writer is able to generate new ideas, explore different perspectives, and overcome their creative block. ChatGPT provides a fresh and innovative perspective on the writer's ideas, pushing them to think outside the box and consider new possibilities.

ChatGPT can also help brainstorm in other fields, such as business, science, and technology. For example, a business owner could use ChatGPT to generate new ideas for product development or marketing campaigns.

A scientist could use ChatGPT to explore new research questions and hypotheses. A technology developer could use ChatGPT to develop new ideas for software development or user interfaces.

ChatGPT can be a valuable tool for individuals and teams looking to generate creative ideas, explore new possibilities, and overcome creative blocks.

ChatGPT can help people think more creatively, generate new ideas, and overcome challenges in their work and personal lives by providing a unique perspective on brainstorming.

# Example 6: Math and Science

ChatGPT is capable of solving very advanced math and physics problems from basic arithmetic to more complex problems in algebra, calculus, geometry, and statistics, among others.

This is excellent for research and solving tricky problems.

Here is its response to *solve a physics problem*

Of course! Here's a simpler problem related to kinematics:

Problem: A ball is thrown vertically upward with an initial velocity of 20 m/s. Find the maximum height the ball reaches.

Solution:

We can use the following kinematic equation to find the maximum height:

$v^2 = u^2 + 2as$

where:
v = final velocity (0 m/s, since the ball comes to a stop at its highest point)
u = initial velocity (20 m/s)
a = acceleration due to gravity (-9.81 m/s², negative since it acts downward)
s = displacement (the maximum height we need to find)

Rearranging the equation to solve for 's':

$s = (v^2 - u^2) / (2a)$

Substituting the values:

$s = (0^2 - 20^2) / (2 * -9.81)$
$s \approx 20.4$ meters

The maximum height the ball reaches is approximately 20.4 meters.

## Use Case 2: Creative

*Use ChatGPT to generate creative ideas and further passions and pursuits.*

ChatGPT has a wide range of creative applications that can inspire, entertain, and facilitate artistic expression.

These are some of its most amusing uses.

Some of examples include:

### Storytelling

ChatGPT can help you generate captivating stories, develop engaging plots, create memorable characters, and even suggest intriguing twists, allowing you to explore new ideas and enhance your narrative skills.

### Poetry and Songwriting

The AI can assist you in writing poems or song lyrics in various styles and formats, offering unique word choices, rhyming schemes, and evocative imagery to fuel your creative process.

### Art and Design Ideas

ChatGPT can offer suggestions for visual art projects, including themes, concepts, and techniques to explore in your artistic endeavors.

### Brainstorming

Whether you're seeking ideas for a marketing campaign, a product name, or a creative project, ChatGPT can generate a wealth of innovative concepts to spark your imagination.

### Screenwriting and Dialogue

The AI can help you craft authentic dialogue for plays, screenplays, or other forms of dramatic writing, providing natural-sounding conversations between characters and enhancing your script's overall impact.

### Humor and Wordplay

ChatGPT can create puns, jokes, riddles, and other forms of wordplay to bring levity and wit to your writing or simply entertain you.

### Creative Problem Solving

The AI can offer alternative perspectives and innovative solutions to challenges you may face in various fields, encouraging out-of-the-box thinking and fostering a creative mindset.

# Example 1: Storytelling and Writing

ChatGPT's storytelling and writing abilities can greatly assist you in the creative process, whether you're an aspiring writer or an experienced author.

Some of the key capabilities that make ChatGPT a valuable tool for storytelling and writing include:

1.  **Idea generation**: ChatGPT can help you brainstorm unique and engaging story ideas, prompts, and themes, providing inspiration and a solid foundation for your creative writing projects.

2.  **Character development**: The AI can aid you in creating well-rounded characters by suggesting character traits, backgrounds, motivations, and relationships, contributing to the depth and realism of your narrative.

3.  **Plot development**: ChatGPT can offer guidance on constructing compelling plotlines and proposing interesting conflicts, resolutions, and plot twists that keep readers engaged and invested in your story.

4.  **Scene and setting descriptions**: The AI can generate vivid, immersive descriptions of scenes and settings, enhancing the atmosphere and mood of your narrative and helping readers visualize your story world.

5.  **Dialogue generation**: ChatGPT can craft authentic, natural-sounding dialogues between characters, capturing their unique voices and personalities and adding dynamism to your story.

6.  **Writing style and tone**: The AI can adapt its writing style and tone to match your preferences or specific genres, ensuring

that your story's language and narrative voice are consistent and appealing to your target audience.

7. **Editing and revision assistance**: ChatGPT can help you refine your drafts by identifying areas for improvement, such as grammar, punctuation, sentence structure, and word choice, ensuring your writing is polished and effective.

8. **Overcoming writer's block**: Whenever you feel stuck or unsure of how to proceed, ChatGPT can provide suggestions, prompts, or alternative story paths to help you overcome writer's block and maintain your creative momentum.

Here's an example of ChatGPT's response to *come up with some ideas for a children's book with a walrus as a main character*

1. "Wally the Walrus and the Sea of Adventure": Wally the Walrus embarks on a thrilling underwater journey to find the legendary Coral Castle. Along the way, he befriends various sea creatures who teach him valuable lessons about friendship, bravery, and teamwork.

2. "The Great Walrus Detective": Wally the Walrus is the greatest detective in the Arctic Ocean. With his keen sense of smell and unmatched problem-solving skills, Wally and his trusty sidekick, Penny the Puffin, solve mysteries and help fellow marine animals in need.

3. "Wally's Wonderful Whiskers": Wally the Walrus has the longest, most amazing whiskers in the Arctic. When his whiskers suddenly start to shed, Wally embarks on a quest to discover the cause and learn the true value of inner beauty and self-confidence.

4. "Wally the Walrus: Time Traveler": Wally discovers a magical seashell that allows him to travel through time. He visits different historical periods and meets fascinating sea creatures from the past, learning important lessons about history and change.

5. "The Walrus and the Iceberg Race": Wally the Walrus and his friends compete in the annual Iceberg Race, an exciting Arctic event that tests their speed, agility, and teamwork. Through perseverance and camaraderie, Wally and his friends learn the importance of sportsmanship and friendship.

# You could even ask ChatGPT to generate chapters for that book:

 Sure! Here are some possible chapter titles for the book "Wally the Walrus and the Sea of  Adventure":

1. A Surprising Discovery: Wally and his friends stumble upon a hidden map that leads to the Coral Castle.
2. The Journey Begins: Wally and his friends embark on a perilous underwater journey, facing treacherous currents and fierce predators.
3. The Coral City: The adventurers finally reach the Coral Castle, a magnificent underwater city filled with wonders and surprises.
4. Friends in Need: When one of their own is in danger, Wally and his friends must use their wits and courage to rescue them from harm.
5. A Mysterious Riddle: Wally and his friends come across a puzzling riddle that might hold the key to uncovering a great treasure.
6. A Race Against Time: The adventurers face a daunting challenge as they try to outrun a menacing school of sharks and reach safety before it's too late.
7. The Shadow of Doubt: Wally starts to doubt his abilities as a leader, but his friends remind him of the importance of trust, teamwork, and perseverance.
8. A Lesson in Forgiveness: When a past mistake comes back to haunt one of their friends, Wally and his friends learn about the power of forgiveness and redemption.
9. The Final Battle: The adventurers face their biggest challenge yet as they confront a mighty foe and fight for the fate of the Coral Castle and all its inhabitants.
10. The Return Home: After a long and exhausting journey, Wally and his friends return home, richer in experience and friendship, and ready for their next adventure.

Once you have your book concept, use ChatGPT to draft the content. ChatGPT can:

- Generate dialogues, descriptions, and narrative elements.
- Receive suggestions to improve or expand your content.

Let's ask it to write a dialogue between Wally and Penny, characters given in example 2 "The Great Walrus Detective":

Wally the Walrus: (yawning) Good morning, Penny! What a beautiful day in the Arctic, isn't it?

Penny the Puffin: (chirping) It sure is, Wally! I've been flying around, and the ice is sparkling like a million diamonds. What do you have planned for today?

Wally the Walrus: Well, I was thinking of exploring that new ice cave we spotted yesterday. Care to join me?

Penny the Puffin: (excited) Absolutely! I've been curious about that cave too. Who knows what fascinating secrets it might hold!

Wally the Walrus: (nodding) That's the spirit, Penny! We'll make a great team, just like always.

Penny the Puffin: (smiling) I couldn't agree more, Wally. We're the perfect duo for this adventure!

Wally the Walrus: (grinning) Alright, let's grab our gear and set off. And don't forget your trusty flashlight, Penny.

Penny the Puffin: (chuckling) You know me too well, Wally. I've got it right here. Let's go uncover the mysteries of the ice cave!

As Wally the Walrus and Penny the Puffin prepared for their exciting adventure, they knew that, together, they could face any challenge the ice cave had in store for them.

What if we want to take it a step further and attempt to generate images for our book?

### Leverage DALL-E and Mid-Journey AI For Creating Illustrations

With your content in place, it's time to create the illustrations for your book. DALL-E, an AI tool from OpenAI, is designed to generate visual content based on textual descriptions.

Mid-Journey AI is another image-generation tool that can be utilized to create diverse illustrations.

To learn about Mid-Journey, search about it on Google, or simply ask ChatGPT how to sign up and use it. In a nutshell, these tools work similarly to ChatGPT, but you describe what image you want to generate.

Here is Mid-Journey's output to *Wally the Walrus is basking in the sun on a rocky shore, his massive body sprawled out lazily on the warm rocks. The waves of the ocean are lapping at his sides, and a flock of seagulls are flying overhead, squawking loudly. Wally is looking out at the vast expanse of the sea, his wise eyes filled with curiosity and a sense of adventure. In the distance, an enormous iceberg is visible, glittering in the sunlight, and Wally wonders what new secrets and wonders might be hidden beneath the surface of the Arctic Ocean.*

You can iterate this process until you achieve the desired illustrations for your book.

### Refine content and illustrations

After creating the text and illustrations, review the content and visuals to ensure they align with your initial vision.

Make any necessary adjustments to the text using ChatGPT or tweak the illustrations by providing more specific descriptions to DALL-E and Mid-Journey AI.

### Combine text and illustrations

Now that you have the content and illustrations, it's time to combine them.

You can use any layout software or platform to arrange your text and images in a visually appealing manner, making sure to maintain a consistent style throughout your book.

As we can see, it's entirely possible to create an illustrated book almost entirely with AI.

# Example 2: Travel Planning

ChatGPT can be a useful tool for travel planning, offering a range of capabilities to help you create detailed itineraries, discover hidden gems, and optimize your travel experience.

Some of the essential abilities that make ChatGPT a valuable resource for travel planning include:

1. **Destination research**: ChatGPT can provide information on popular travel destinations, including local customs, culture, cuisine, and attractions. The AI can also recommend off-the-beaten-path destinations and suggest activities that match your interests.

2. **Travel logistics**: The AI can assist you in planning transportation, such as car rentals, trains, or buses, and help you create detailed travel schedules, including maps and directions. You'll still need to check these.

3. **Language translation**: ChatGPT can help you overcome language barriers by offering real-time translations of foreign languages, making it easier to communicate with locals and navigate unfamiliar places.

4. **Weather and climate information:** The AI can provide up-to-date weather forecasts and climate data, helping you pack and plan accordingly.

5. **Safety and health information**: ChatGPT can offer you safety tips, health recommendations, and vaccination requirements for your travel destination, ensuring you stay safe and healthy during your trip. Don't 100% rely on it for this, use it as a guide.

6. **Local currency and money exchange**: The AI can provide information on currency exchange rates, local banking options, and payment methods, making it easier to manage your finances while abroad.

Here's some of ChatGPT's response to *write me a 4-day itinerary for visiting Italy*

 Title: A 4-Day Itinerary for Visiting Italy

Introduction:

Italy is a country rich in history, culture, and natural beauty. It is nearly impossible to cover all the magnificent attractions in just four days. However, this itinerary will help you make the most of your short visit, focusing on Rome, Florence, and Venice – three iconic Italian cities that offer a taste of the country's art, history, and cuisine.

Day 1: Rome
Morning:

* Arrive in Rome and check into your accommodation.
* Start your day with a visit to the Colosseum, one of the most famous landmarks in the world. Be sure to book tickets in advance to avoid long queues.
* Walk to the nearby Roman Forum and Palatine Hill, which offer a glimpse into ancient Rome's daily life.

Afternoon:

* Stop for lunch at a local trattoria and savor some authentic Roman pasta, such as cacio e pepe or carbonara.
* Head to Vatican City and explore St. Peter's Basilica, the largest church in the world. Don't forget to admire Michelangelo's Pietà and the stunning view from the dome.
* Visit the Vatican Museums, where you can see the Sistine Chapel and its famous ceiling frescoes painted by Michelangelo.

Evening:

You can get more granular than that. Here's ChatGPT's response to *provide me a costed itinerary of visiting across Peru and north Brazil, including journey times and rough costs, for 14-days*

 Sure, here's a possible costed itinerary for a 14-day trip across Peru and North Brazil:

Day 1-3: Lima, Peru

- Flight from home country to Lima
- Visit historical landmarks such as the Huaca Pucllana, the Basilica and Convent of San Francisco, and the Plaza Mayor
- Explore the neighborhoods of Barranco and Miraflores
- Average daily cost: $100-150 per person

Day 4-6: Cusco and Machu Picchu, Peru

- Take a flight from Lima to Cusco
- Visit the Sacred Valley and the town of Aguas Calientes
- Hike or take a train to Machu Picchu, one of the world's most renowned ancient sites
- Average daily cost: $150-200 per person

Day 7-9: Amazon Rainforest, Peru

- Fly from Cusco to Puerto Maldonado
- Take a boat trip to the Tambopata National Reserve, a vast rainforest with a rich biodiversity of flora and fauna
- Stay at an eco-lodge and participate in guided hikes and wildlife watching tours
- Average daily cost: $200-250 per person

Day 10-12: Rio de Janeiro, Brazil

## Example 3: Hobbies and DIY

ChatGPT can assist with various hobbies and DIY projects, providing guidance, inspiration, and problem-solving support.

Here are some examples of how ChatGPT can help you pursue your hobbies, interests and passions:

1. **Creative writing**: ChatGPT can provide writing prompts, character development ideas, and plot twists, helping you generate new story ideas and overcome writer's block.

2. **Cooking and baking**: The AI can offer recipe suggestions, cooking tips, and dietary advice, helping you prepare delicious and healthy meals and desserts.

3. **Gardening and landscaping**: ChatGPT can provide gardening tips, plant care advice, and landscaping ideas, helping you create beautiful and sustainable outdoor spaces.

4. **Crafting and DIY:** The AI can offer step-by-step tutorials, product recommendations, and creative inspiration for various crafts and DIY projects, such as sewing, knitting, woodworking, and more.

5. **Photography and videography**: ChatGPT can provide technical tips, composition suggestions, and editing advice for your photography and videography projects, helping you create compelling and visually stunning media content.

6. **Music and art**: The AI can provide you with musical theory guidance, instrument playing techniques, and art style inspiration, helping you develop your skills and creativity in these areas.

7. **Fitness and health:** ChatGPT can offer exercise routines, healthy lifestyle suggestions, and medical information, helping you stay fit and healthy and achieve your fitness goals.

Here's ChatGPT's response to *give me 5 home DIY projects for a rainy day*

 Sure! Here are 5 DIY projects you can do at home on a rainy day:

1. Repurpose Old Furniture: Take an old piece of furniture you no longer use or like and give it new life. Sand it down, paint it a new color, or add some new hardware. With a little bit of creativity, you can transform something old into something new and exciting.
2. Create a Gallery Wall: Use the blank wall space in your home to create a gallery of your favorite photos, art prints, or posters. You can use frames of different shapes and sizes to create a unique and visually appealing display.
3. Build a Bookshelf: Create a new space for your favorite books by building your own bookshelf. You can use wood boards, metal brackets, or even repurpose old crates or pallets. This is a great project for both beginners and experienced DIYers.
4. Make a Terrarium: Build your own mini garden inside a glass container by creating a terrarium. You can use succulents, moss, rocks, and other natural materials to create a beautiful and low-maintenance indoor garden.
5. Design Your Own Decorative Pillows: Add a pop of color and personality to your home by designing your own decorative pillows. You can use fabric paint, stencils, or even create your own design using iron-on transfer paper. This is a fun and easy project that can be completed in an afternoon.

**Now we can ask for step-by-step guidance on one we like, such as designing our own decorative pillows** *give me a step by step for idea 5*

 Sure! Here's a step-by-step guide for designing your own decorative pillows:

Materials:

* Plain throw pillows
* Fabric paint
* Paintbrushes
* Stencils
* Iron-on transfer paper (optional)
* Iron

Steps:

1. Choose the pillow cover: Select plain, neutral-colored pillow covers as a base for your design. You can purchase these at any home decor or craft store.
2. Pick a design: Choose a design for your pillow. You can use stencils, freehand drawing, or even create your own design on your computer using graphic design software.
3. Set up your workspace: Cover your workspace with newspaper or a drop cloth to protect it from paint spills. Set out your pillow covers, paint, paintbrushes, stencils, and any other materials you will be using.
4. Paint your design: Using your paintbrush and fabric paint, carefully paint your design onto the pillow cover. If you are using stencils, secure them in place with tape before painting. Let the paint dry completely before moving on to the next step.
5. Add details: Once the base layer of paint is dry, you can add details or shading to your design using different colors or shades of paint.
6. Iron on transfer paper (optional): If you created your own design on your computer, print it onto iron-on transfer paper and follow the instructions to transfer it onto your pillow

# Example 4: Recipes

ChatGPT can write full recipes, though these are worth checking whether you start gathering everything together.

Here's part of ChatGPT's response to *write a recipe for roast chicken*

 Here's a simple recipe for a classic roast dinner featuring roast chicken, roast potatoes, and  mixed vegetables. Feel free to adjust the ingredients and portions according to your preferences.

Ingredients:

* 1 whole chicken (about 3-4 lbs)
* 2 lbs potatoes, peeled and quartered
* 1 lb mixed vegetables (e.g., carrots, green beans, Brussels sprouts)
* 1/4 cup olive oil
* 2 tbsp unsalted butter, softened
* 2 cloves garlic, minced
* 1 tbsp fresh rosemary, chopped (or 1 tsp dried)
* 1 tbsp fresh thyme, chopped (or 1 tsp dried)
* Salt and pepper, to taste

Instructions:

1. Preheat the oven to 425°F (220°C).
2. Prepare the chicken:
   a. Remove the giblets and pat the chicken dry with paper towels.
   b. Season the cavity with salt and pepper.
   c. In a small bowl, mix together the softened butter, minced garlic, chopped rosemary, and thyme. Rub this mixture evenly under the skin and over the outside of the chicken.
   d. Truss the chicken by tying the legs together with kitchen twine and tucking the wings under the body.

# Example 5: Songwriting and Poetry

ChatGPT can write convincing songs and poetry.

Here's its response to *Write a rap about a penguin*

*(Verse 1)*
*Yo, listen up, it's time to tell a tale,*
*'Bout a penguin that's beyond the pale,*
*He's black and white and full of swag,*
*He's the coolest bird that you ever had.*

*(Chorus)*
*Penguin, penguin, he's the man,*
*Swimming in the sea and walking on land,*
*He's got the moves, he's got the style,*
*Penguin, penguin, he'll make you smile.*

*(Verse 2)*
*He waddles on the ice with a beat in his step,*
*Diving in the water with no regrets,*
*He's got a slick suit and a beak that's sharp,*
*He's the king of the cold and he's got the heart.*

*(Chorus)*
*Penguin, penguin, he's the man,*
*Swimming in the sea and walking on land,*
*He's got the moves, he's got the style,*
*Penguin, penguin, he'll make you smile.*

*(Bridge)*
*He may not fly, he may not soar,*
*But he's got a spirit you can't ignore,*
*He's a survivor in a world so cold,*
*He's got the heart of a champion, bold and bold.*

*(Verse 3)*
*He's got a colony that he calls his own,*
*And he'll protect it 'til the day he's grown,*
*He's a social creature with a lot to say,*
*And he'll strut his stuff every single day.*

*(Chorus)*
*Penguin, penguin, he's the man,*
*Swimming in the sea and walking on land,*
*He's got the moves, he's got the style,*
*Penguin, penguin, he'll make you smile.*

*(Outro)*
*So don't underestimate this little bird,*
*He's got more than you ever heard,*
*He's a symbol of resilience and strength,*
*And he'll keep on waddling 'til the end of length.*

And here's the output to *write a Limerick and Haiku poem about a misty mountain*

## Limerick:

*There once was a mountain so misty,*
*Its peak in the clouds was quite twisty.*
*Climbers would scale,*
*Telling their tale,*
*Of the summit's allure, oh so risky!*

## Haiku:

*Misty mountain shroud,*
*Silent whispers, nature's voice,*
*Eternal secrets.*

## Use Case 3: Business

ChatGPT can be used for a variety of business purposes, including customer service, marketing, sales, and operations.

Here are some examples of how ChatGPT can be utilized to enhance your business:

1. **Resume writing**: ChatGPT can assist with creating resumes and cover letters that stand out to potential employers. The AI can suggest relevant skills, experiences, and achievements to include in your resume and provide feedback on the overall tone and format.

2. **Career development**: ChatGPT can assist with career development by providing insights on job market trends, suggesting relevant job opportunities, and offering advice on professional development.

3. **Personal finance**: ChatGPT can assist with personal finance by providing budgeting advice, investment recommendations, and financial planning tips. The AI can also assist with tax preparation and filing.

4. **Time management**: ChatGPT can assist with time management by providing productivity tips, creating personalized schedules, and offering suggestions for time-saving techniques.

5. **Language learning**: ChatGPT can assist with language learning by providing conversational practice, vocabulary quizzes, and grammar exercises. The AI can also provide cultural insights and tips on language immersion.

# Example 1: Resume Writing

Let's take a look at resume writing first.

1. **Resume formatting:** ChatGPT can suggest resume templates and formatting guidelines that are visually appealing and easy to read. It can help you organize your content clearly and concisely, ensuring that your resume is easy to navigate.

2. **Content creation**: In addition, ChatGPT can assist with content creation by suggesting relevant skills, experiences, and achievements to include in your resume. It can analyze job descriptions and match them with your own experiences, helping you tailor your resume to specific job opportunities.

3. **Language usage**: When it comes to writing, ChatGPT can assist with language usage by suggesting word choice, tone, and grammar. The AI can help you avoid common resume mistakes, such as using jargon or cliches, and offer advice on how to write compelling descriptions of your experiences and accomplishments.

4. **Keywords**: ChatGPT can assist with including keywords relevant to the job you are applying for. For example, it can analyze job descriptions and suggest keywords that match the job requirements, helping you pass through automated resume screening processes.

5. **Proofreading**: Finally, ChatGPT can assist with proofreading your resume, helping you catch any spelling or grammatical errors. For instance, ChatGPT can also provide feedback on your resume's overall tone and readability.

## Here's ChatGPT's response to *write me a job application for a job in machine learning at OpenAI*

 [Your Name]

[Your Address]

[City, State, Zip Code]

[Your Email Address]

[Today's Date]

[OpenAI Hiring Manager's Name]

OpenAI

[Company Address]

[City, State, Zip Code]

Dear [Hiring Manager's Name],

I am writing to express my sincere interest in the Machine Learning position at OpenAI. As a highly skilled and motivated individual with a strong background in artificial intelligence, machine learning, and data analysis, I am confident that my expertise aligns with the values and goals of OpenAI. Your organization's commitment to shaping the future of AI in a manner that benefits humanity greatly resonates with me, and I am eager to contribute to your groundbreaking research.

Throughout my academic and professional career, I have gained extensive knowledge in various machine learning techniques such as deep learning, natural language processing, and computer vision. As a recent graduate from [Your University] with a [Your Degree], I have successfully completed projects that involved implementing state-of-the-art machine learning algorithms, such as GPT and BERT, to solve complex problems. In addition to my academic achievements, my internships at [Company Name 1] and [Company Name 2] have equipped me with practical skills in data preprocessing, model training, and evaluation, as well as experience with TensorFlow, PyTorch, and other essential ML frameworks.

# Example 2: Business Ideas

ChatGPT can assist with generating business ideas by offering insights, resources, and guidance to help individuals identify their strengths, passions, and market opportunities.

Here are some ways ChatGPT can help with business idea generation:

1. **Brainstorming**: ChatGPT can assist with brainstorming sessions to help you generate new ideas for business ventures. The AI can ask you questions about your interests, experiences, and goals, and offer suggestions based on your responses.

2. **Market research**: For market research, ChatGPT can help you conduct market research to identify areas of opportunity in the market. The AI can analyze market trends, consumer behavior, and competition to help you identify gaps in the market that you can fill with your business idea.

3. **SWOT analysis**: ChatGPT can help you conduct a SWOT analysis to evaluate the strengths, weaknesses, opportunities, and threats of your business idea. The AI can assist with identifying potential challenges and offering solutions to mitigate them.

4. **Business planning**: When it comes to planning. ChatGPT can assist with business planning, including creating a business plan, developing a marketing strategy, and identifying funding sources. The AI can also provide insights into legal requirements and regulations that need to be followed.

5. **Mentorship**: Finally, ChatGPT can offer mentorship and coaching to guide you through the process of starting and growing a business. The AI can provide feedback on your progress, offer advice on best practices, and help you overcome any challenges you may face.

Here's ChatGPT's response to *generate 5 business ideas trending in 2023*

1. Personal Health and Wellness Platforms: As health awareness and the demand for personalized wellness plans continue to rise, a business offering personalized health coaching, nutrition, and fitness advice through an online platform or mobile app can capitalize on this trend. Integrating wearable technologies, AI-powered analytics, and virtual reality can create a unique and immersive experience for users.

2. Sustainable Living Solutions: With growing concerns about climate change and environmental degradation, businesses focusing on eco-friendly products and services are in high demand. Offering sustainable alternatives to everyday items, such as biodegradable packaging, zero-waste products, or energy-efficient home solutions, can attract environmentally conscious consumers.

3. Remote Work Solutions and Consultancy: The shift towards remote and flexible work has become more permanent for many businesses, creating a demand for remote work solutions and consulting services. A business that provides tools, strategies, and support for effective remote work, including team collaboration, project management, and employee wellness, can thrive in this market.

4. EdTech for Lifelong Learning: The need for continuous learning and skill development is more important than ever. A business offering innovative educational technology solutions, such as micro-learning platforms, virtual workshops, or AI-powered adaptive learning systems, can cater to professionals seeking to stay relevant in a rapidly evolving job market.

5. Urban Farming and Vertical Agriculture: As urban populations continue to grow and the demand for locally sourced, fresh produce increases, urban farming and vertical agriculture solutions present a unique business opportunity. Establishing vertical farms in urban areas, utilizing hydroponics, aeroponics, or aquaponics systems, can provide a sustainable and efficient way to grow fresh produce and contribute to local food systems.

# Example 3: Social Media Content Creation

Social media writing and production is key to running a business today.

ChatGPT can assist with content creation for social media platforms in several ways:

1. **Topic and keyword suggestions:** ChatGPT can provide ideas for topics and keywords that are relevant to your audience and industry. You can provide a general topic, and the AI can suggest specific subtopics or angles to focus on. Additionally, ChatGPT can analyze the language used by your target audience to identify the most relevant keywords to include in your posts.

2. **Content formats**: ChatGPT can suggest various content formats to make your social media content more engaging, such as lists, how-to guides, infographics, and videos. ChatGPT can recommend the best format based on your content goals and the preferences of your target audience.

3. **Headline and caption generation**: When it comes to writing, ChatGPT can help create attention-grabbing headlines and captions for your social media posts. For example, the AI can analyze the language used by your target audience and suggest phrasing and word choices that are likely to be more engaging and memorable.

4. **Tone and voice**: ChatGPT can assist with establishing a consistent tone and voice for your social media content. For instance, the AI can help you identify your brand's personality and values and suggest language that reflects these qualities.

5. **Hashtag suggestions**: For hashtags, ChatGPT can suggest relevant hashtags to include in your social media posts. The AI can analyze the language used by your target audience and suggest the most popular and relevant hashtags to use.

Here's ChatGPT's response to *write me social media posts for a bakery business*

1. Introducing our newest sweet treat: the Triple Chocolate Explosion! 🍫 Indulge in layers of rich chocolate cake, creamy chocolate ganache, and a velvety chocolate mousse. It's the perfect dessert for chocolate lovers everywhere! 😋 #TripleChocolateExplosion #BakeryDelights #ChocolateHeaven

2. Rise and shine, it's croissant time! 🥐 Start your morning off right with our freshly baked, buttery croissants. Pair it with a steaming cup of coffee, and you're all set for a fantastic day! #MorningMotivation #CroissantLove #BakeryBreakfast

3. Do you have a birthday, anniversary, or special event coming up? 🎉 Let us make it memorable with our custom cakes, tailored to your taste and style! Get in touch with us to bring your dream cake to life. 🎂 #CustomCakes #CelebrateWithUs #BakeryMagic

4. It's #SourdoughSaturday! 🍞 Stop by our bakery today to grab a loaf of our homemade sourdough bread. Made with love and natural fermentation, it's the perfect base for sandwiches, toast, or just to enjoy on its own! 😊 #SourdoughLove #ArtisanBread #BakeryFresh

5. Who says you can't have dessert first? 🍩 Treat yourself to our delectable donuts, available in a variety of flavors to satisfy your sweet tooth. Go ahead, you deserve it! 😊 #DonutDelights #BakeryTreats #DessertFirst

# Example 4: Market Research

As an AI language model, ChatGPT's market research capabilities can provide users with insights and general trends within various industries based on the data and knowledge available up to September 2021.

While ChatGPT cannot provide real-time data or updates, it can offer the following types of information:

1. **Industry trends**: ChatGPT can provide information on historical and current trends in various industries, such as technology, healthcare, finance, and more.

2. **Market analysis**: Once trends and industries are identified, ChatGPT can help users understand the competitive landscape, market segmentation, and potential growth opportunities within specific markets.

3. **Consumer behavior:** ChatGPT can offer insights into consumer preferences, purchasing habits, and other factors influencing their decisions in various industries.

4. **SWOT analysis**: ChatGPT can help users identify strengths, weaknesses, opportunities, and threats for companies or industries.

5. **Key players**: ChatGPT can provide information on major companies, their products and services, and their strategies within specific industries.

# Here's ChatGPT's response to *Conduct market research on the CBD market in 2022*

I am an AI language model and cannot access real-time data, but I can provide you with general insights and trends about the CBD market up until my knowledge cutoff in September 2021. If you are looking for specific data or updated figures, I recommend checking the latest industry reports or market research studies.

That being said, in 2021 the global CBD market was experiencing significant growth, with projections for continued expansion into 2022. The following trends were observed leading up to 2022:

1. Market growth: The CBD market had been experiencing rapid growth, with increasing demand for CBD products due to their potential health benefits and the easing of regulations in many countries. Projections estimated that the global CBD market could reach $23.6 billion by 2025.
2. Increased product variety: As the market expanded, companies were introducing a wide range of CBD products, such as oils, tinctures, capsules, edibles, beverages, topicals, and vape products. This diversification allowed consumers to choose products that best fit their preferences and needs.
3. Legalization and regulation: The ongoing legalization and regulation of cannabis in various countries, including the United States and Canada, positively impacted the CBD market. As more countries legalized the use of CBD, the market was expected to grow further in 2022.
4. Consumer awareness: Greater awareness of the potential health benefits of CBD, such as its anti-inflammatory, analgesic, and anxiolytic properties, contributed to increased consumer demand for CBD products.

# Example 5: Career Development

ChatGPT is a useful and objective tool for individuals seeking assistance with career development.

By offering valuable information and guidance, it can support people in various aspects of their professional growth:

1. **Career exploration**: ChatGPT can provide insights into different professions, industries, and job roles, helping users identify suitable career paths based on their interests, skills, and goals.

2. **Skill development**: To develop your skills, ChatGPT can offer recommendations on relevant skills, certifications, and training programs that can enhance users' employability and career prospects.

3. **Resume and cover letter guidance**: For writing resumes, ChatGPT can provide tips on creating effective resumes and cover letters, tailored to specific job applications or industries.

4. **Interview preparation**: For interviews, ChatGPT can help users prepare for job interviews by providing commonly asked questions, advice on effective responses, and guidance on interview etiquette.

5. **Networking tips**: ChatGPT can offer suggestions on how to build professional networks, both online and offline, which can be essential for career advancement.

6. **Personal branding**: ChatGPT can provide insights on how to develop a personal brand, which can be beneficial for job seekers and professionals looking to establish themselves in their industry.

7. **Job search strategies**: If you're looking for a job, ChatGPT can help users identify effective job search strategies, including the use of job boards, social media, and professional networks, to optimize their job hunt.

8. **Career advancement**: ChatGPT can offer advice on strategies for career growth, such as seeking new challenges, taking on leadership roles, and pursuing professional development opportunities.

Here is ChatGPT's response to *what can I do as a career for an ex-teacher?*

 There are numerous alternative career paths available for ex-teachers who are looking to leverage their skills and experiences in new ways. Here are some options to consider:

1. Corporate trainer: Ex-teachers can use their expertise in education and communication to design and deliver training programs for businesses, helping employees develop new skills and improve their performance.

2. Educational consultant: Ex-teachers can work with schools, districts, or educational organizations to provide guidance on curriculum development, instructional strategies, and educational policy.

3. Curriculum developer: Ex-teachers can create instructional materials, lesson plans, and assessments for educational institutions, textbook publishers, or e-learning platforms.

4. Tutoring or coaching: Ex-teachers can offer private tutoring or academic coaching services to students, either in-person or online, helping them improve in specific subjects or prepare for exams.

5. Nonprofit work: Ex-teachers can apply their skills to work with nonprofit organizations focused on education, youth development, or community outreach, in roles such as program coordinator or project manager.

6. Human resources: Ex-teachers can transition into human resources roles, leveraging their interpersonal and communication skills in areas such as recruitment, employee development, or employee relations.

7. Instructional designer: Ex-teachers can design and develop online courses, multimedia materials, and interactive learning experiences for e-learning platforms or corporate training programs.

8. Career counselor: Ex-teachers can use their knowledge of education and experience in guiding students to help individuals explore career options, develop professional skills, and navigate the job market.

# Example 6: Business Productivity

One of the most promising applications of ChatGPT for businesses is in the area of productivity.

ChatGPT can be used to automate tasks that would otherwise be time-consuming or tedious, freeing up employees to focus on higher-value tasks. Here are some potential applications for ChatGPT in business:

1. **Personalized marketing**: ChatGPT can help businesses create content that resonates with their customers on a deeper level. By analyzing customer data, ChatGPT can generate personalized emails, social media posts, or product recommendations that reflect customers' interests and preferences.

2. **Predictive analytics**: With ChatGPT, businesses can gain insights into customer behavior and market trends. By analyzing data, ChatGPT can help businesses make data-driven decisions and predict future trends, enabling them to stay ahead of the competition.

3. **Language translation**: If you cooperate with customers across different languages, ChatGPT can help businesses communicate effectively with customers from different places.

4. **Content creation**: ChatGPT can help businesses generate high-quality content that engages and informs their customers. By analyzing data and generating insights, ChatGPT can create valuable content for websites, social media, or other marketing materials, saving businesses time and effort.

5. **Chatbot development**: If you have programming or development knowledge, ChatGPT can help businesses create chatbots that can provide instant customer support and assistance. Chatbots can be programmed to answer frequently asked questions, provide product information, or help customers with issues, reducing the workload on customer service representatives.

6. **Sales forecasting**: If you have data, ChatGPT can help businesses forecast future sales and revenue based on historical data and market trends. By providing businesses with real-time insights, ChatGPT can help them make informed decisions and plan for future growth.

7. **Legal research**: ChatGPT can help businesses stay up-to-date with legal requirements and regulations by analyzing legal documents and generating insights. ChatGPT can help businesses make informed decisions and reduce legal risks by providing them with valuable insights into legal issues.

## Use Case 4: Technical

ChatGPT can be incredibly helpful for various technical tasks related to coding and other related activities.

Here's a more detailed and engaging description of how ChatGPT can be of use for technical purposes:

1. **Custom code examples**: ChatGPT can provide tailored code snippets in various programming languages, such as Python, JavaScript, Java, C++, and more, based on the user's requirements and context.

2. **Code logic clarification**: If you encounter confusing or complex code, ChatGPT can help by explaining the underlying logic, syntax, and functionality in a clear and accessible manner.

3. **Debugging assistance**: If you face issues with their code, ChatGPT can help identify potential causes and solutions, as well as suggest improvements to enhance code quality and functionality.

4. **Best practices guidance**: ChatGPT can provide advice on coding best practices, sharing insights on design patterns, coding conventions, and optimization techniques to help users elevate their code quality.

5. **Algorithm support:** If you need help with specific problems, ChatGPT can assist in designing or selecting the most suitable algorithm, while explaining its complexities and trade-offs.

6. **Library and framework recommendations**: ChatGPT can suggest relevant libraries or frameworks for users' projects and provide guidance on effectively integrating and using them.

7. **Project idea generation**: ChatGPT can spark creativity by suggesting coding project ideas based on their interests and skill level.

8. **Learning resource suggestions**: If you want to learn a new programming language or technology, ChatGPT can recommend tutorials, courses, or books tailored to their needs.

9. **Code review**: ChatGPT can act as a code reviewer, examining users' code to provide feedback on potential improvements, as well as identifying any bugs or issues that may arise.

10. **Technical concept explanations**: ChatGPT can help people grasp complex technical concepts, such as data structures, algorithms, computer networks, and more, by breaking them down into understandable components.

## Example 1: Debugging

Debugging is the process of identifying, diagnosing, and resolving errors, issues, or anomalies in a software program or code.

These errors, commonly known as bugs, can be related to syntax, logic, performance, or unexpected behavior.

Debugging is a crucial part of software development, as it helps ensure that the code runs correctly, efficiently, and as intended.

As an AI language model, ChatGPT can assist in debugging by:

1. **Error analysis**: ChatGPT can help you understand the error messages you encounter, explaining the possible causes and suggesting potential solutions.

2. **Code examination**: ChatGPT can review your code and identify possible issues such as syntax errors, logical errors, or misuse of functions, libraries, or programming constructs.

3. **Best practices**: ChatGPT can provide guidance on coding best practices to prevent common bugs, improve code quality, and enhance maintainability.

4. **Troubleshooting suggestions**: ChatGPT can offer general troubleshooting tips and strategies to help you diagnose and resolve issues more effectively.

5. **Performance optimization**: ChatGPT can help identify performance bottlenecks and suggest ways to optimize your code, resulting in more efficient and faster-running programs.

6. **Error prevention**: ChatGPT can advise on strategies to write more robust code that anticipates and handles potential issues, reducing the likelihood of bugs occurring in the future.

Here's an example:

 Sure! Let's consider a common debugging scenario involving a Python script. Suppose you  have the following code snippet with an issue:

```python
def add_numbers(a, b):
    result = a + b
    return result

number1 = 5
number2 = "10"

total = add_numbers(number1, number2)
print(total)
```

When you run this code, you encounter an error:

```bash
TypeError: unsupported operand type(s) for +: 'int' and 'str'
```

ChatGPT can help you identify the problem and suggest a solution. In this case, the issue is caused by trying to add a number (`int`) and a string (`str`). The variable `number2` is assigned a string value, while `number1` is assigned an integer value.

To fix this issue, you can convert `number2` to an integer before passing it to the `add_numbers` function. Here's the corrected code:

# Example 2: Generating Code

As an AI language model, ChatGPT can generate code for various programming projects by understanding your requirements and providing relevant code snippets or examples in the desired programming language.

Here's how ChatGPT can assist in generating code for projects:

1. **Understand the requirements**: Clearly explain the goals, objectives, and functionality you want to achieve in your project. This helps ChatGPT understand the context and tailor the code generation accordingly.

2. **Specify the language**: Mention the programming language you want the code to be generated in, such as Python, JavaScript, Java, C++, etc. ChatGPT has knowledge of various languages and can generate code accordingly.

3. **Code snippets**: ChatGPT can provide code snippets or examples to help you implement specific functionality or solve particular problems. You can combine and modify these snippets to build your project.

4. **Libraries and frameworks**: ChatGPT can recommend libraries or frameworks that can help you implement desired functionality in your project more efficiently. Additionally, it can guide how to use them effectively.

5. **Code structure and organization**: ChatGPT can suggest best practices for structuring and organizing your code to make it more readable, maintainable, and scalable.

6. **Design patterns**: ChatGPT can recommend design patterns that suit your project's requirements, ensuring that your code follows industry standards and is easier to extend or modify in the future.

7. **Algorithm suggestions**: ChatGPT can provide direction on selecting appropriate algorithms or data structures to optimize your project's performance and meet specific requirements.

Here's ChatGPT's response to being asked to write code for Pacman:

 Creating a complete Pac-Man game requires a significant amount of code and is too extensive to provide in a single response. However, I can help you get started by providing a high-level overview of the game components and suggesting a game development library to use.

Pac-Man is a 2D maze arcade game, and the Pygame library is a popular choice for developing 2D games in Python. To start, you will need to install Pygame:

```
pip install pygame
```

Here's a high-level overview of the game components:

1. Initialize the game window and screen.
2. Load the maze, images, and sounds.
3. Create classes for the game objects (Pac-Man, ghosts, pellets, etc.).
4. Implement the main game loop, which includes:
   a. Handling user input (keyboard events)
   b. Updating the game objects (movement, collision detection, scoring)
   c. Drawing the game objects on the screen
   d. Managing game states (start, play, pause, game over)

# Example 3: Algorithm Support

Algorithm support refers to helping users understand, select, design, and implement algorithms to solve specific problems.

As an AI language model, ChatGPT can provide recommendations on choosing the right algorithm based on the problem at hand, explain how the algorithm works, discuss its time and space complexity, and help implement it in code.

Here are some examples of how ChatGPT can offer algorithm support:

1. **Sorting algorithms**: Suppose you need help choosing the right sorting algorithm for your project. ChatGPT can guide you by comparing different sorting algorithms, such as Quick Sort, Merge Sort, and Bubble Sort, based on their average-case time complexity, worst-case time complexity, space complexity, and stability. It can also provide code examples and explanations on how to implement the chosen sorting algorithm in your preferred programming language.

2. **Graph algorithms**: If you're working on a project that involves graphs, ChatGPT can help you understand and choose the appropriate graph algorithm to solve your problem. For example, if you need to find the shortest path between two nodes in a weighted graph, ChatGPT can explain the Dijkstra's algorithm, its time complexity, and how it compares to other shortest path algorithms such as Bellman-Ford or A*. Additionally, it can help you implement Dijkstra's algorithm in your code.

3. **Search algorithms**: In a scenario where you need to search for a specific element in a data structure, ChatGPT can help you choose and understand the right search algorithm. If you have a sorted list, it can explain how the Binary Search algorithm works, its time complexity, and how it compares to other search algorithms like Linear Search. It can also provide advice on implementing Binary Search in your desired programming language.

4. **Machine learning algorithms**: If you're working on a machine learning project and need help selecting the right algorithm, ChatGPT can provide guidance based on your specific problem and dataset. For example, suppose you're dealing with a classification problem. In that case, it can compare and explain various classification algorithms like Logistic Regression, Support Vector Machines, and Decision Trees, discussing their strengths, weaknesses, and appropriate use cases. It can also help you implement the chosen algorithm using popular machine learning libraries like scikit-learn or TensorFlow.

# How To Make Money With ChatGPT

ChatGPT has a myriad of uses, but it's perhaps unsurprising that many people are trying to harness it to make money.

Here are 50 very raw ideas of how to make money with ChatGPT:

1. Develop an AI-powered customer service chatbot for businesses.
2. Create an AI language model-based writing assistant for content creators.
3. Build an AI-powered scheduling and reminder service.
4. Develop an AI-based personal finance advisor.
5. Create an AI-powered automated data entry service.
6. Build an AI-based news aggregator service.
7. Develop an AI-powered quiz and survey tool.
8. Create an AI-based resume and cover letter builder.
9. Build an AI-based lead qualification tool.
10. Develop an AI-powered e-commerce product recommendation service.
11. Create an AI-based stock market analysis tool.
12. Build an AI-based music playlist recommendation service.
13. Develop an AI-powered recipe recommendation service.
14. Create an AI-based travel itinerary planning tool.
15. Build an AI-based weather forecast service.
16. Develop an AI-powered fitness and nutrition planner.
17. Create an AI-based language learning tool.
18. Build an AI-based automated content creation service.
19. Develop an AI-powered personality test and analysis tool.

20. Create an AI-based online tutoring service.

21. Build an AI-based project management tool.

22. Develop an AI-powered legal document generation service.

23. Create an AI-based news summarization tool.

24. Build an AI-based plagiarism checker.

25. Develop an AI-powered meditation and mindfulness app.

26. Create an AI-based writing prompt generator.

27. Build an AI-based business plan generator.

28. Develop an AI-powered online reputation management tool.

29. Create an AI-based life coaching service.

30. Build an AI-based chatbot for mental health support.

31. Develop an AI-powered transcription service.

32. Create an AI-based virtual interior design service.

33. Build an AI-based smart home automation service.

34. Develop an AI-powered financial planning tool.

35. Create an AI-based AI chatroom for education and training.

36. Build an AI-based online marketplace for freelance services.

37. Develop an AI-powered voice-to-text transcription service.

38. Create an AI-based legal advice platform.

39. Build an AI-based stock portfolio management tool.

40. Develop an AI-powered project proposal generator.

41. Create an AI-based fitness tracker and personalized workout planner.

42. Build an AI-based investment recommendation service.

43. Develop an AI-powered chatbot for HR and employee benefits support.

44. Create an AI-based voice-activated home assistant for seniors and disabled individuals.

45. Build an AI-based chatbot for academic writing and research support.

46. Develop an AI-powered interior design consultation and product recommendations.
47. Create an AI-based automated email marketing and lead generation.
48. Build an AI-powered chatbot for personalized financial planning and retirement advice.
49. Develop an AI-based virtual fashion assistant for wardrobe planning and outfit coordination.
50. Create an AI-based chatbot for mental wellness and meditation support.

Now, let's dig down into a few of the better examples:

## 1: Develop a ChatGPT-Powered Virtual Assistant Business

As an entrepreneur, you can create a virtual assistant service that utilizes ChatGPT's powerful language processing capabilities.

This could involve developing a platform where customers can subscribe to your service, which offers them access to an AI-powered personal assistant that can handle tasks like scheduling, research, content creation, and customer support.

To make this successful, focus on:
- Identifying target markets, such as small businesses, entrepreneurs, or busy professionals, who would benefit from a virtual assistant.
- Building a user-friendly interface for your platform that makes it easy for clients to access and manage their virtual assistant.
- Offering customizable plans based on the level of assistance needed to cater to various budgets and requirements.

- Continuously improving your service by gathering feedback from customers and implementing necessary updates.

## 2: Create ChatGPT-Powered Chatbots for Businesses:

Develop customizable chatbots that use ChatGPT's advanced language processing capabilities to provide businesses with automated customer support, sales, and lead generation services.

These chatbots can handle various tasks like answering customer inquiries, providing product recommendations, and guiding users through the sales process.

To make this successful, focus on:
- Researching the industries that could benefit most from chatbot services and targeting them as your primary customers.
- Creating customizable templates and conversation flows to cater to different business needs.
- Offering integration options with popular messaging platforms and CRM systems.
- Actively promoting your chatbot services through targeted marketing strategies and showcasing successful case studies.

## 3: Develop ChatGPT-Powered Educational Tools

Leverage ChatGPT's capabilities to create educational tools and platforms that help students and professionals learn new skills, practice problem-solving, and engage with course material.

These tools can include AI-driven tutoring services, interactive learning platforms, or personalized study materials.

To make this successful, focus on:

- Identifying the areas where AI-powered educational tools can add the most value, such as language learning, coding, or standardized test preparation.
- Designing engaging and user-friendly interfaces that facilitate learning and knowledge retention.
- Partnering with educational institutions or online learning platforms to promote your products and services.
- Gathering user feedback to continuously improve your educational tools and adapt to changing needs.

## 4: Create ChatGPT-Driven Marketing Automation Tools

Develop marketing automation tools that utilize ChatGPT's language processing capabilities to help businesses manage their marketing campaigns more efficiently.

These tools include email marketing, social media scheduling, ad copy generation, and audience targeting.

To make this successful, focus on:
- Researching the most common marketing challenges faced by businesses and designing tools that address those specific needs.
- Creating user-friendly interfaces and customizable templates that make it easy for businesses to manage their marketing campaigns.
- Offering integration with popular marketing platforms and analytics tools to ensure seamless campaign management.
- Actively promoting your marketing automation tools through targeted advertising, partnerships, and industry events.

# In-Depth Example: YouTube Channel

Creating video scripts for a YouTube channel using ChatGPT and automating the video creation process can effectively generate consistent, engaging content. That content can be monetized for ad revenue.

Here's an in-depth example of how you can build and maintain a YouTube channel with this approach:

## Niche Selection

Choose a niche for your YouTube channel that aligns with your interests and expertise. Research the competition, target audience, and potential for growth within that niche.

Identify content gaps or unique angles that you can cover to differentiate your channel.

## Content Strategy

Develop a content strategy that outlines the types of videos you want to create, their format, length, and frequency.

Consider a mix of evergreen content that remains relevant over time and trending topics that capture viewers' interest.

## Generate Video Scripts

Use ChatGPT to create video scripts based on the topics you've chosen. Provide the AI with detailed prompts, outlining the subject, key points, and structure of the video.

You can also use the AI to generate catchy titles and video descriptions that encourage viewers to click on your videos.

## Automate Video Creation

Collaborate with video creation platforms or tools that offer automation capabilities to convert your scripts into engaging videos. Platforms like InVideo, Lumen5, and Renderforest can help you create videos with minimal manual intervention.

Experiment with different video styles, templates, and formats to find the best fit for your channel's brand and audience.

## Edit and Refine Videos

While automation tools can help speed up the video creation process, reviewing and editing the final output is important to ensure it meets your standards.

Use video editing software to polish your videos, add additional elements like transitions or animations, and fine-tune the pacing and structure.

## Optimize Videos for YouTube

Optimize your videos for YouTube by including relevant keywords in your titles, descriptions, and tags.

Create eye-catching custom thumbnails that encourage viewers to click on your videos. Research the best times to publish your content to maximize views and engagement.

## Promote Your Channel

Leverage social media, online communities, and collaborations with other YouTubers to promote your channel and grow your audience.

Engage with your viewers through comments and social media to build a loyal following.

## Monetize Your Channel

Once your channel gains traction, explore various monetization options, such as YouTube's Partner Program, sponsored content, affiliate marketing, and merchandise sales.

Here's an example of how ChatGPT can write a script *write me a script for a DIY channel*

## Title: DIY: Build Your Own Stylish Wooden Coffee Table

## INTRO:

*[Upbeat background music playing]*

*Host: (Smiling) Hi, and welcome back to our DIY channel! Today, we're going to show you how to build your own stylish wooden coffee table that's not only functional but also adds a touch of elegance to your living space. So, grab your tools and let's get started!*

## SCENE 1: Materials and Tools

*Host: Before we begin, let's go over the materials and tools you'll need for this project:*
- *A wooden tabletop (approximately 24" x 48")*
- *4 wooden legs (16" each)*
- *Wood screws (8 x 1-1/4")*

- *Sandpaper (80 and 220 grit)*
- *Wood stain of your choice*
- *Polyurethane finish*
- *Paintbrushes*
- *Screwdriver or drill*
- *Measuring tape*
- *Carpenter's square*
- *Safety goggles and gloves*
- *Now that we have everything ready, let's start building our coffee table!*

## SCENE 2: Prepping the Wood

Host: *First, we need to prep our wooden pieces. Start by sanding the tabletop and legs with 80-grit sandpaper to remove any rough edges. Then, use the 220-grit sandpaper for a smoother finish. (Host demonstrates sanding)*

## SCENE 3: Staining the Wood

Host: *Once your wood is smooth, it's time to apply the wood stain. Choose a color that complements your interior decor. Use a paintbrush to apply an even coat of stain on the tabletop and legs, following the wood grain. Allow the stain to dry according to the manufacturer's instructions. (Host demonstrates staining)*

## SCENE 4: Attaching the Legs

Host: *Now that our stain is dry, it's time to attach the legs. Turn the tabletop upside down and position the legs at each corner, ensuring they are square and evenly spaced. Use a measuring tape and carpenter's square to double-check their alignment. (Host demonstrates positioning legs)*

Next, secure each leg with two wood screws, drilling them diagonally from the leg into the tabletop. Remember to wear safety goggles when using a drill or screwdriver. (Host demonstrates attaching legs)

## SCENE 5: Applying the Finish

Host: With the legs securely attached, let's apply a polyurethane finish to protect the wood and give it a beautiful shine. Using a clean paintbrush, apply a thin, even coat of polyurethane on the tabletop and legs. Allow it to dry, then lightly sand with 220-grit sandpaper. Repeat this process for a total of 2-3 coats, allowing ample drying time between each coat. (Host demonstrates applying finish)

## SCENE 6: The Final Result

Host: (Smiling) And there you have it! Your very own stylish wooden coffee table, built from scratch! Place it in your living room and enjoy the fruits of your labor. It's a perfect addition to any home and a great conversation starter.

## OUTRO:

Host: Thank you for joining us today! If you enjoyed this DIY project, don't forget to like, share, and subscribe to our channel for more fun and creative projects. Leave a comment below and let us know what DIY project you'd like to see next. Until next time, happy crafting!

# Risk and Drawbacks of ChatGPT

**While ChatGPT seems incredible at face value, it is crucial to examine the risks associated with this technology. It's not infallible.**

As AI models become more advanced and integrated into various aspects of our lives, it's essential to ensure that they do not cause harm, reinforce biases, or violate ethical norms.

By understanding the risks of ChatGPT and exploring ways to mitigate them, we can ensure that this technology is used responsibly and for the benefit of society.

OpenAI themselves place great emphasis on people understanding the risks of ChatGPT and AI in general. These tools are not infallible, and they do not know everything.

We can't depend on them to run our lives for us, and must be wary of them affecting our identities as humans.

## Risks of ChatGPT

## 1: Bias and Discrimination

### Sources of Bias

One of the most significant risks associated with ChatGPT is bias and discrimination.

ChatGPT, like other AI models, can amplify existing biases in the data it's trained on. If the training data is biased, the model will learn and replicate those biases, leading to discriminatory or unfair outcomes.

Some sources of bias in ChatGPT include:
- **Selection bias**: The training data may not represent the diversity of people, languages, or cultures, leading to biased or skewed representations of certain groups.
- **Historical bias**: The training data may reflect historical inequalities, stereotypes, or prejudices, perpetuating discriminatory practices.
- **Contextual bias**: The model may not account for the context or intent of the language used, leading to misinterpretations and unfair judgments.

## Consequences of Bias

The consequences of bias in ChatGPT can be severe and far-reaching. If the model perpetuates discrimination or stereotypes, it can harm individuals or communities by reinforcing systemic inequalities or marginalizing certain groups.

ChatGPT can also lead to incorrect or unfair decisions in domains such as hiring, lending, or criminal justice. In extreme cases, bias in AI models can contribute to social unrest or even conflict.

## Case Studies

Several case studies have highlighted the potential for bias in AI models. For example, a study by MIT found that facial recognition technology had higher error rates for people with darker skin tones, leading to unfair outcomes in law enforcement and surveillance.

# 2: Misinformation and Fake News

Another risk associated with ChatGPT is the potential for misinformation and fake news.

ChatGPT can generate human-like responses to natural language prompts, making it possible for malicious actors to use the technology to spread false or misleading information.

Some sources of misinformation in ChatGPT include:
- **Gaps in knowledge**: The model may not have access to all relevant or accurate information, leading to incorrect or incomplete responses.
- **Malicious intent**: The model can be manipulated or hacked to generate false information or propaganda.
- **Lack of context**: The model may not fully understand the context or implications of the language used, leading to misinterpretations or misunderstandings.

## Consequences of Misinformation

The consequences of misinformation and fake news generated by ChatGPT can be significant. It can contribute to public distrust in information sources, erode democratic values, and even incite violence or social unrest.

Misinformation can also harm individuals or organizations by spreading false or damaging information, leading to reputational or financial harm.

## Case Studies

Several case studies have highlighted the potential for misinformation and fake news generated by AI models.

In one example, a team of researchers used GPT-2 to generate fake news articles that were accepted by several major news outlets, highlighting the potential for AI-generated misinformation to spread undetected.

## 3: Privacy and Security

Another risk associated with ChatGPT is privacy and security. ChatGPT requires access to large amounts of data to train and improve its models, raising concerns about data collection and storage.

If the data is not adequately protected or anonymized, it may lead to privacy violations or data breaches.

Some sources of privacy and security risks in ChatGPT include:
- **Data breaches**: The data used to train the model can be hacked or stolen, leading to unauthorized access to sensitive information.
- **Privacy violations**: The model may inadvertently reveal personal or confidential information in generated responses, leading to privacy violations.
- **Data bias**: The data used to train the model may contain sensitive or personally identifiable information, leading to privacy concerns.

### Cyberattacks and Hacking

ChatGPT is also vulnerable to cyberattacks and hacking, which can lead to a range of negative consequences. If the model is hacked or compromised, it could potentially lead to data theft, identity theft, or other malicious activities.

Some sources of cyberattacks and hacking risks in ChatGPT include:

- **Malicious intent**: Attackers may seek to exploit vulnerabilities in the model to cause harm or disruption.
- **Technical vulnerabilities**: The model may contain technical vulnerabilities that can be exploited by attackers.
- **Insider threats**: Internal actors with malicious intent may seek to access or steal data from within the organization or compromise the model's security.

**Case Studies**

Several case studies have highlighted the risks associated with privacy and security in AI models. For example, in 2019, a chatbot developed by Microsoft was found to have stored user data in an unsecured database, leading to privacy violations.

In another example, a team of researchers demonstrated that they could use adversarial attacks to trick AI models, including ChatGPT, into generating misleading or false responses.

## 4: Ethical Concerns

Another risk associated with ChatGPT is the potential for loss of human control and responsibility. As AI models become more advanced, there is a risk that they may operate autonomously or without sufficient human oversight.

If AI takes everyone's jobs, governments won't be able to raise taxes. Society will be threatened.

Some sources of ethical concerns in ChatGPT include:

- **Lack of human oversight**: The model may operate without sufficient human oversight, leading to unintended consequences or harm.

- **Responsibility gaps**: It may be difficult to assign responsibility for negative outcomes of AI models, leading to accountability gaps.
- **Decision-making processes**: The model may be used to make decisions that significantly impact individuals or communities, raising concerns about fairness and justice.

## Accountability and Transparency

ChatGPT also raises concerns about accountability and transparency. If the model's decision-making processes are opaque or difficult to understand, assessing its performance and ensuring accountability for negative outcomes can be challenging.

Some sources of ethical concerns in ChatGPT include:
- **Lack of transparency**: The model's decision-making processes may be difficult to understand or explain, leading to concerns about bias or discrimination.
- **Lack of accountability**: Assigning accountability for negative outcomes of AI models may be challenging, leading to accountability gaps.
- **Unintended consequences**: The model may have unintended consequences or impacts that are difficult to anticipate or control.

## Case Studies

Several case studies have highlighted the potential for ethical concerns in AI models. For example, in 2018, Amazon abandoned a recruitment tool that was biased against women, highlighting the risks of AI models perpetuating discriminatory practices.

In another example, law enforcement's use of AI-powered facial recognition technology by law enforcement has raised concerns about civil liberties and human rights.

## Summary of Risks

Everyone should be aware of the risks and drawbacks of AI. The sooner we can build a collective understanding of them, the better.

Here are the main points to be aware of:
- ChatGPT is an AI-powered language model that can generate human-like responses to natural language prompts. While this technology has the potential to transform the way we communicate and interact with machines, it also comes with certain risks and drawbacks.
- One major risk associated with ChatGPT is the potential for bias and discrimination. If the model perpetuates stereotypes or biases, it can harm individuals or communities by reinforcing systemic inequalities. This can lead to incorrect or unfair decisions in areas such as hiring, lending, or criminal justice.
- Another risk is the potential for misinformation and fake news generated by ChatGPT. Malicious actors can use this technology to spread false or misleading information, which can contribute to public distrust in information sources, erode democratic values, and even incite violence or social unrest.
- ChatGPT also raises concerns about privacy and security. The model requires access to large amounts of data to train and improve its models, which raises concerns about data collection and storage. If the data is not adequately protected or anonymized, it can lead to privacy violations or data breaches. Additionally, ChatGPT is vulnerable to cyberattacks

and hacking, which can lead to data theft, identity theft, or other malicious activities.

- Finally, ChatGPT raises ethical concerns around human control and responsibility. As AI models become more advanced, there is a risk that they may operate autonomously or without sufficient human oversight, leading to unintended consequences or harm. It can also be challenging to assign responsibility for negative outcomes of AI models, leading to accountability gaps.

- To mitigate these risks, it is essential to develop robust mitigation strategies that address issues such as data collection and training, algorithmic fairness and interpretability, fact-checking and verification, data protection and anonymization, cybersecurity measures and best practices, human oversight and governance, and ethical guidelines and standards.

- By being aware of these risks and taking proactive steps to mitigate them, we can help ensure that AI models like ChatGPT are used responsibly and ethically, benefiting society as a whole.

# Final Comments

In the captivating journey through the world of ChatGPT, we have explored the layers and the far-reaching implications of this powerful technology.

ChatGPT is hugely useful, and these examples are a snippet of what you can do with the tool.

**With trial, error and experimentation, you'll be able to wield ChatGPT to assist you in a vast array of tasks.**

As we conclude, it's crucial to acknowledge the ever-evolving nature of artificial intelligence and its potential to reshape human experiences.

We must strive to create an inclusive future where AI-powered tools like ChatGPT are used not just for the betterment of a select few, but for the collective good of all humanity.

We encourage readers to remain vigilant, informed, and engaged with the AI community.

By fostering a culture of collaboration and open discussion, we can steer the development of ChatGPT and other AI innovations towards a future that is ethical, transparent, and truly beneficial to us all.

In the words of Alan Turing, "We can only see a short distance ahead, but we can see plenty there that needs to be done."

# ChatGPT FAQ

**Q: How does ChatGPT generate context-aware responses?**
A: ChatGPT uses a technique called Transformer architecture, which relies on self-attention mechanisms to understand the context of the input text. It's trained on a vast corpus of text from the internet, learning patterns and relationships between words and phrases. This knowledge helps it generate context-aware and human-like responses.

**Q: Can ChatGPT understand multiple languages?**
A: Yes, ChatGPT has been trained on multilingual data, which enables it to understand and generate text in various languages. However, its proficiency may vary depending on the language and the amount of training data available for that particular language.

**Q: What are the limitations of ChatGPT?**
A: Some limitations of ChatGPT include:
1. Producing plausible-sounding but incorrect or nonsensical answers.
2. Sensitivity to input phrasing, which may result in different responses for slight rephrasing.
3. Tendency to be verbose and overuse certain phrases.
4. Struggling with ambiguous queries and not asking clarifying questions.
5. Potential to generate biased or offensive content.

**Q: How can I stay updated on the latest developments in ChatGPT and AI?**
A: To stay updated on ChatGPT and other AI developments, you can follow OpenAI's blog, social media channels, and subscribe to relevant newsletters. Additionally, participating in AI conferences, webinars, and online forums can help you stay informed about the latest advancements in the field.

**Q: What does the future hold for ChatGPT and similar AI models?**
**A**: The future of ChatGPT and similar AI models likely involves further improvements in performance, increased versatility, and broader applications across various industries.

As AI research advances, we can expect these models to become more accurate, context-aware, and capable of generating creative outputs. The ongoing development of AI ethics and safety measures will also play a crucial role in shaping the future of these models.

**Q: Can we expect real-time human-AI collaboration using ChatGPT in the future?**
**A**: Yes, as the technology continues to advance, real-time human-AI collaboration will become more feasible. This collaboration may manifest in various forms, such as AI-powered co-writing tools, brainstorming assistants, or real-time language translators. Such applications will enable humans and AI to work together more seamlessly, enhancing productivity and creativity.

**Q: How might ChatGPT help in closing the digital divide?**
**A**: ChatGPT and similar AI models have the potential to bridge the digital divide by providing equal access to information, educational resources, and services across languages and regions. By offering multilingual support, these models can help break language barriers, enabling people from different backgrounds to access and share knowledge. Additionally, AI-powered tools can assist in developing localized content, further narrowing the digital divide.

**Q: Will ChatGPT eventually replace human-generated content?**
**A**: While ChatGPT and similar AI models are becoming increasingly proficient at generating content, they are not expected to entirely replace human-generated content.

Instead, these AI tools will likely augment human capabilities, assisting in content creation and enhancing productivity. Human creativity, emotions, and experiences will continue to play a vital role in shaping unique and engaging content.

# EXCLUSIVE BONUS

## Scan the QR code and get 33 highly useful Chat GPT prompts for free!

# Disclaimer

This book contains opinions and ideas of the author and is meant to teach the reader informative and helpful knowledge while due care should be taken by the user in the application of the information provided. The instructions and strategies are possibly not right for every reader and there is no guarantee that they work for everyone. Using this book and implementing the information/recipes therein contained is explicitly your own responsibility and risk. This work with all its contents, does not guarantee correctness, completion, quality or correctness of the provided information. Misinformation or misprints cannot be completely eliminated.

Printed in Great Britain
by Amazon

24073742R00065